Māori Cookbook

Authentic Recipes

UNCOVER THE RICH AND DIVERSE FLAVORS OF NEW ZEALAND

AMARA E. KAIHE

MĀORI COOKBOOK FOR TWO
Uncover the Rich and Diverse Flavors of New Zealand.

© Amara E. Kaihe
© E.G.P. Editorial

Printed in USA.
ISBN-13: 9798391790525

The "Māori Cookbook" is a comprehensive guide to traditional Māori cuisine, showcasing the rich cultural heritage and diverse flavors of this region.

This cookbook offers a unique insight into the ingredients, cooking techniques, and customs of Māori cuisine, making it an essential tool for anyone looking to delve into the world of Māori food.

With a focus on authenticity, the book provides recipes and instructions for dishes that have been passed down for generations and continue to be enjoyed by families today.

The recipes are easy to follow and are accompanied by clear and concise instructions, making it accessible to both experienced and novice cooks.

So if you're looking to expand your culinary horizons and discover the rich tastes and aromas of Māori cuisine, this cookbook is the perfect resource.

Let's discover the wonders of Māori cuisine!

TABLE OF CONTENTS

STARTERS

KINA PAIPAI

Ingredients:

- 1 Kina (Sea Urchin)
- Lemon Juice
- Olive Oil
- Salt
- Pepper

Instructions:

1. Open the Kina and remove the roe.

2. Place the roe in a bowl and add lemon juice, olive oil, salt, and pepper to taste.

3. Mix well and serve as a starter.

TUNA SASHIMI

Ingredients:

- 300g Sashimi-grade Tuna
- Soy Sauce
- Wasabi
- Pickled Ginger

Instructions:

1. Cut the Tuna into thin slices.

2. Serve the Tuna slices with soy sauce, wasabi, and pickled ginger on the side.

3. Dip the Tuna in the sauce and enjoy.

KAKARIKI TAPENADE

Ingredients:

- 1 cup Green Olives
- 1/2 cup Fresh Parsley
- 1 Garlic Clove
- 1 tbsp Capers
- 2 tbsp Olive Oil
- 1 Lemon, juiced

Instructions:

1. In a food processor, add the green olives, parsley, garlic, capers, olive oil, and lemon juice.

2. Pulse until a smooth paste forms.

3. Serve the tapenade with crackers or sliced baguette.

PIPI KAIRANGI

Ingredients:

- 1 cup Pipi (New Zealand Clams)
- 1/2 cup White Wine
- 1 Garlic Clove, minced
- 1 tbsp Butter
- 1 tbsp Olive Oil
- Salt
- Pepper

Instructions:

1. In a pan, heat the olive oil and butter over medium heat.

2. Add the minced garlic and cook until fragrant.

3. Add the white wine to the pan and let it simmer.

4. Add the pipi to the pan and cover with a lid.

5. Cook until the pipi have opened, about 5-7 minutes.

6. Season with salt and pepper to taste.

7. Serve the pipi with crusty bread to soak up the sauce.

PAUA FRITTERS

Ingredients:

- 1 cup Paua (Abalone) Meat
- 1 cup Flour
- 1 tsp Baking Powder
- 1 Egg
- 1/2 cup Milk
- 1 tsp Salt
- Pepper
- Oil for frying

Instructions:

1. In a bowl, mix together the flour, baking powder, salt, and pepper.

2. In another bowl, beat the egg and mix in the milk.

3. Add the wet ingredients to the dry ingredients and mix until a batter forms.

4. Stir in the Paua meat.

5. Heat oil in a pan over medium heat.

6. Spoon the batter into the hot oil and fry until golden brown, about 2-3 minutes on each side.

7. Serve the Paua fritters hot with a lemon wedge.

RAUKUMARA RANGOON

Ingredients:

- 1 cup Raukumara (Crayfish) Meat
- 1/2 cup Cream Cheese
- 1 Green Onion, chopped
- 1 tsp Soy Sauce
- 1/4 tsp Garlic Powder
- Wonton Wrappers
- Oil for frying

Instructions:

1. In a bowl, mix together the Raukumara meat, cream cheese, green onion, soy sauce, and garlic powder.

2. Place a spoonful of the mixture in the center of a wonton wrapper.

3. Fold the wrapper in half to form a triangle and press the edges to seal.

4. Repeat with the remaining wrappers and filling.

5. Heat oil in a pan over medium heat.

6. Fry the Rangoon until golden brown, about 2-3 minutes on each side.

7. Serve the Raukumara Rangoon hot with sweet chili sauce or soy sauce for dipping.

TĀHUHU KŌUKA

Ingredients:

- 1 head Broccoli
- 2 Garlic Cloves, minced
- 1 tsp Olive Oil
- 1 tsp Lemon Juice
- Salt
- Pepper

Instructions:

1. Cut the broccoli into florets.

2. In a pan, heat the olive oil over medium heat.

3. Add the minced garlic and cook until fragrant.

4. Add the broccoli to the pan and stir to coat with the garlic and oil.

5. Cover the pan and let the broccoli steam until tender, about 5-7 minutes.

6. Remove the pan from heat and drizzle with lemon juice.

7. Season with salt and pepper to taste.

8. Serve the Tāhuhu Kōuka as a side dish.

HEIHEI PARAOA

Ingredients:

- 300g Chicken Breasts
- 1 tsp Paprika
- 1 tsp Garlic Powder
- 1 tsp Salt
- Pepper
- 1 tbsp Olive Oil

Instructions:

1. Cut the chicken into bite-sized pieces.

2. In a bowl, mix together the paprika, garlic powder, salt, and pepper.

3. Add the chicken to the bowl and toss to coat with the spices.

4. In a pan, heat the olive oil over medium heat.

5. Add the chicken to the pan and cook until golden brown and cooked through, about 10-12 minutes.

6. Serve the Heihei Paraoa as a main dish or in a wrap or sandwich.

KERERU PATE

Ingredients:

- 1 cup Kereru (Wood Pigeon) Meat
- 1/2 cup Butter

- 1 Onion, chopped
- 2 Garlic Cloves, minced
- 1 tsp Thyme
- 1 tsp Salt
- Pepper

Instructions:

1. In a pan, melt the butter over medium heat.

2. Add the chopped onion and minced garlic to the pan and cook until softened.

3. Add the Kereru meat to the pan and break it up into small pieces.

4. Cook the Kereru until no longer pink, about 5-7 minutes.

5. Season with thyme, salt, and pepper to taste.

6. Remove the pan from heat and let the mixture cool.

7. Transfer the mixture to a food processor and pulse until smooth.

8. Serve the Kereru pate with crackers or sliced baguette.

TUNA AND POTATO PATTIES

Ingredients:

- 1 cup Tuna, drained and flaked
- 1 cup Mashed Potatoes
- 1 Egg
- 1 Green Onion, chopped
- 1 tsp Lemon Juice

- 1 tsp Salt
- Pepper
- Oil for frying

Instructions:

1. In a bowl, mix together the flaked tuna, mashed potatoes, egg, green onion, lemon juice, salt, and pepper.

2. Shape the mixture into small patties.

3. Heat oil in a pan over medium heat.

4. Fry the patties until golden brown, about 2-3 minutes on each side.

5. Serve the Tuna and Potato Patties hot with lemon wedges and tartar sauce.

SNACKS

ROASTED KUMARA CHIPS

Ingredients:

- 4 medium-sized kumara
- 2 tablespoons olive oil
- Salt and pepper to taste

Instructions:

1. Preheat the oven to 200°C. Line a large baking sheet with parchment paper.

2. Wash and peel the kumara and cut into thin rounds or fries.

3. In a large bowl, toss the kumara with olive oil, salt, and pepper until evenly coated.

4. Arrange the kumara in a single layer on the prepared baking sheet and bake for 20-25 minutes, or until crispy and golden brown.

5. Serve immediately and enjoy your Roasted Kumara Chips!

FRIED TARO ROOT

Ingredients:

- 1 large taro root
- 1 cup all-purpose flour
- 1 teaspoon salt

- 1 teaspoon baking powder
- 1/2 cup water
- Vegetable oil for frying

Instructions:

1. Wash and peel the taro root and cut into thin slices or wedges.

2. In a large bowl, mix together the flour, salt, and baking powder. Gradually add water and mix until a smooth batter forms.

3. Heat the vegetable oil in a deep pan or wok over medium heat until hot.

4. Dip each taro slice into the batter, making sure it is evenly coated. Carefully place the battered taro into the hot oil and fry until golden brown, about 3-5 minutes per side.

5. Remove from the oil and place on a paper towel to drain excess oil. Serve immediately with your favorite dipping sauce and enjoy your Fried Taro Root!

TARO FRITTERS

Ingredients:

- 1 large taro root
- 1 cup all-purpose flour
- 1 egg
- 1/2 cup milk
- 1 teaspoon baking powder
- Salt and pepper to taste
- Vegetable oil for frying

Instructions:

1. Wash and peel the taro root and grate into a large bowl.

2. Add the flour, egg, milk, baking powder, salt, and pepper to the bowl.

3. Mix all the ingredients together until well combined.

4. Heat the vegetable oil in a deep pan or wok over medium heat until hot.

5. Using a spoon, drop spoonfuls of the batter into the hot oil and fry until golden brown, about 3-5 minutes per side.

6. Remove from the oil and place on a paper towel to drain excess oil. Serve immediately and enjoy your Taro Fritters!

FRIED BREADFRUIT

Ingredients:

- 1 medium-sized breadfruit
- 1 cup all-purpose flour
- 1 teaspoon salt
- 1 teaspoon baking powder
- 1/2 cup water
- Vegetable oil for frying

Instructions:

1. Wash and peel the breadfruit and cut into thin slices or wedges.

2. In a large bowl, mix together the flour, salt, and baking powder. Gradually add water and mix until a smooth batter forms.

3. Heat the vegetable oil in a deep pan or wok over medium heat until hot.

4. Dip each breadfruit slice into the batter, making sure it is evenly coated. Carefully place the battered breadfruit into the hot oil and fry until golden brown, about 3-5 minutes per side.

5. Remove from the oil and place on a paper towel to drain excess oil. Serve immediately and enjoy your Fried Breadfruit!

KŪMARA SLICE

Ingredients:

- 2 medium-sized kumara
- 2 tablespoons olive oil
- 1/4 cup all-purpose flour
- 1 egg
- 1/4 cup milk
- 1 teaspoon baking powder
- Salt and pepper to taste

Instructions:

1. Preheat the oven to 200°C. Line a large baking sheet with parchment paper.

2. Wash and peel the kumara and slice into thin rounds or fries.

3. In a large bowl, mix together the flour, egg, milk, baking powder, salt, and pepper. Gradually add the sliced kumara and toss until evenly coated.

4. Arrange the kumara in a single layer on the prepared baking sheet and bake for 20-25 minutes, or until crispy and golden brown.

5. Serve immediately and enjoy your Kūmara Slice!

TARAKIHI FRITTERS

Ingredients:

- 1 pound tarakihi fish fillets
- 1 cup all-purpose flour
- 1 egg
- 1/2 cup milk
- 1 teaspoon baking powder
- Salt and pepper to taste
- Vegetable oil for frying

Instructions:

1. Rinse the tarakihi fillets and cut into bite-sized pieces.

2. In a large bowl, mix together the flour, egg, milk, baking powder, salt, and pepper. Gradually add the tarakihi pieces and mix until well coated.

3. Heat the vegetable oil in a deep pan or wok over medium heat until hot.

4. Using a spoon, drop spoonfuls of the batter into the hot oil and fry until golden brown, about 3-5 minutes per side.

5. Remove from the oil and place on a paper towel to drain excess oil. Serve immediately and enjoy your Tarakihi Fritters!

FRIED CASSAVA

Ingredients:

- 2 medium-sized cassava
- 1 cup all-purpose flour
- 1 teaspoon salt
- 1 teaspoon baking powder
- 1/2 cup water
- Vegetable oil for frying

Instructions:

1. Wash and peel the cassava and cut into thin slices or wedges.

2. In a large bowl, mix together the flour, salt, and baking powder. Gradually add water and mix until a smooth batter forms.

3. Heat the vegetable oil in a deep pan or wok over medium heat until hot.

4. Dip each cassava slice into the batter, making sure it is evenly coated. Carefully place the battered cassava into the hot oil and fry until golden brown, about 3-5 minutes per side.

5. Remove from the oil and place on a paper towel to drain excess oil. Serve immediately and enjoy your Fried Cassava!

FRIED PLANTAINS

Ingredients:

- 2 ripe plantains
- 1 cup all-purpose flour
- 1 teaspoon salt
- 1 teaspoon baking powder
- 1/2 cup water
- Vegetable oil for frying

Instructions:

1. Peel the plantains and cut into thin slices or wedges.

2. In a large bowl, mix together the flour, salt, and baking powder. Gradually add water and mix until a smooth batter forms.

3. Heat the vegetable oil in a deep pan or wok over medium heat until hot.

4. Dip each plantain slice into the batter, making sure it is evenly coated. Carefully place the battered plantain into the hot oil and fry until golden brown, about 3-5 minutes per side.

5. Remove from the oil and place on a paper towel to drain excess oil. Serve immediately and enjoy your Fried Plantains!

KUMARA AND CARROT FRITTERS

Ingredients:

- 2 medium-sized kumara
- 2 medium-sized carrots

- 1 cup all-purpose flour
- 1 egg
- 1/2 cup milk
- 1 teaspoon baking powder
- Salt and pepper to taste
- Vegetable oil for frying

Instructions:

1. Wash, peel, and grate the kumara and carrots into a large bowl.

2. Add the flour, egg, milk, baking powder, salt, and pepper to the bowl with the grated kumara and carrots and mix until well combined.

3. Heat the vegetable oil in a deep pan or wok over medium heat until hot.

4. Using a spoon, drop spoonfuls of the batter into the hot oil and fry until golden brown, about 3-5 minutes per side.

5. Remove from the oil and place on a paper towel to drain excess oil. Serve immediately and enjoy your Kumara and Carrot Fritters!

SWEET POTATO WEDGES

Ingredients:

- 4 medium-sized sweet potatoes
- 2 tablespoons olive oil
- Salt and pepper to taste

Instructions:

1. Preheat the oven to 200°C. Line a large baking sheet with parchment paper.

2. Wash and peel the sweet potatoes and cut into wedges or fries.

3. In a large bowl, toss the sweet potatoes with olive oil, salt, and pepper until evenly coated.

4. Arrange the sweet potatoes in a single layer on the prepared baking sheet and bake for 20-25 minutes, or until crispy and golden brown.

5. Serve immediately and enjoy your Sweet Potato Wedges!

SOUPS

TĪTĪ (MUTTONBIRD) SOUP

Ingredients:

- 1 kg Tītī (Muttonbird) meat
- 1 large onion, chopped
- 3 cloves of garlic, minced
- 2 large carrots, chopped
- 2 celery stalks, chopped
- 1 tsp dried thyme
- 1 tsp dried rosemary
- 6 cups of chicken broth
- 1 cup of water
- Salt and pepper to taste

Instructions:

1. Rinse and clean the Tītī meat, removing any feathers and fat.

2. In a large pot, heat some oil and sauté the onion, garlic, carrots, and celery until soft.

3. Add the Tītī meat to the pot and cook until browned on all sides.

4. Add the thyme, rosemary, chicken broth, water, salt, and pepper to the pot.

5. Bring the mixture to a boil, then reduce the heat and let it simmer for 1-2 hours or until the meat is tender.

6. Serve hot and enjoy the authentic taste of Tītī soup.

TARO AND KUMARA SOUP

Ingredients:

- 1 large taro, peeled and chopped
- 2 large kumara, peeled and chopped
- 1 large onion, chopped
- 2 cloves of garlic, minced
- 1 tsp turmeric powder
- 1 tsp cumin powder
- 1 tsp coriander powder
- 6 cups of chicken broth
- 1 cup of water
- Salt and pepper to taste

Instructions:

1. In a large pot, heat some oil and sauté the onion and garlic until soft.

2. Add the taro and kumara to the pot and cook for a few minutes until slightly browned.

3. Add the turmeric, cumin, coriander, chicken broth, water, salt, and pepper to the pot.

4. Bring the mixture to a boil, then reduce the heat and let it simmer for 20-30 minutes or until the vegetables are tender.

5. Use a blender or immersion blender to blend the mixture until smooth.

6. Serve hot and enjoy the authentic taste of Taro and Kumara soup.

HĀPUKA AND PUMPKIN SOUP

Ingredients:

- 500g Hāpuka fish fillets, diced
- 1 large pumpkin, peeled and chopped
- 1 large onion, chopped
- 3 cloves of garlic, minced
- 1 tsp paprika powder
- 1 tsp dried thyme
- 6 cups of fish broth
- 1 cup of water
- Salt and pepper to taste

Instructions:

1. In a large pot, heat some oil and sauté the onion and garlic until soft.

2. Add the pumpkin to the pot and cook for a few minutes until slightly browned.

3. Add the paprika, thyme, fish broth, water, salt, and pepper to the pot.

4. Bring the mixture to a boil, then reduce the heat and let it simmer for 20-30 minutes or until the pumpkin is tender.

5. Add the Hāpuka fish to the pot and cook for 5-7 minutes or until fully cooked.

6. Use a blender or immersion blender to blend the mixture until smooth.

7. Serve hot and enjoy the authentic taste of Hāpuka and Pumpkin soup.

TARAKIHI CHOWDER

Ingredients:

- 500g Tarakihi fish fillets, diced
- 2 large potatoes, peeled and chopped
- 1 large onion, chopped
- 3 cloves of garlic, minced
- 1 cup of corn kernels
- 1 tsp dried thyme
- 6 cups of fish broth
- 1 cup of heavy cream
- Salt and pepper to taste

Instructions:

1. In a large pot, heat some oil and sauté the onion and garlic until soft.

2. Add the potatoes to the pot and cook for a few minutes until slightly browned.

3. Add the corn, thyme, fish broth, salt, and pepper to the pot.

4. Bring the mixture to a boil, then reduce the heat and let it simmer for 20-30 minutes or until the potatoes are tender.

5. Add the Tarakihi fish to the pot and cook for 5-7 minutes or until fully cooked.

6. Stir in the heavy cream and heat until warm, but do not let it boil.

7. Serve hot and enjoy the authentic taste of Tarakihi Chowder.

CRAYFISH CHOWDER

Ingredients:

- 500g crayfish tail meat, diced
- 2 large potatoes, peeled and chopped
- 1 large onion, chopped
- 3 cloves of garlic, minced
- 1 cup of corn kernels
- 1 tsp paprika powder
- 6 cups of fish broth
- 1 cup of heavy cream
- Salt and pepper to taste

Instructions:

1. In a large pot, heat some oil and sauté the onion and garlic until soft.

2. Add the potatoes to the pot and cook for a few minutes until slightly browned.

3. Add the corn, paprika, fish broth, salt, and pepper to the pot.

4. Bring the mixture to a boil, then reduce the heat and let it simmer for 20-30 minutes or until the potatoes are tender.

5. Add the crayfish tail meat to the pot and cook for 5-7 minutes or until fully cooked.

6. Stir in the heavy cream and heat until warm, but do not let it boil.

7. Serve hot and enjoy the authentic taste of Crayfish Chowder.

PUHA AND PORK SOUP

Ingredients:

- 500g pork belly, diced
- 1 bunch of puha (sow thistle), chopped
- 1 large onion, chopped
- 3 cloves of garlic, minced
- 2 large carrots, chopped
- 2 celery stalks, chopped
- 6 cups of chicken broth
- 1 cup of water
- Salt and pepper to taste

Instructions:

1. In a large pot, heat some oil and sauté the onion, garlic, carrots, and celery until soft.

2. Add the pork belly to the pot and cook until browned on all sides.

3. Add the puha, chicken broth, water, salt, and pepper to the pot.

4. Bring the mixture to a boil, then reduce the heat and let it simmer for 1-2 hours or until the pork is tender.

5. Serve hot and enjoy the authentic taste of Puha and Pork soup.

CLAM CHOWDER

Ingredients:

- 1 kg of clams, cleaned and removed from the shells
- 2 large potatoes, peeled and chopped

- 1 large onion, chopped
- 3 cloves of garlic, minced
- 1 cup of corn kernels
- 1 tsp dried thyme
- 6 cups of fish broth
- 1 cup of heavy cream
- Salt and pepper to taste

Instructions:

1. In a large pot, heat some oil and sauté the onion and garlic until soft.

2. Add the potatoes to the pot and cook for a few minutes until slightly browned.

3. Add the corn, thyme, fish broth, salt, and pepper to the pot.

4. Bring the mixture to a boil, then reduce the heat and let it simmer for 20-30 minutes or until the potatoes are tender.

5. Add the clams to the pot and cook for 5-7 minutes or until they have opened up and are fully cooked.

6. Stir in the heavy cream and heat until warm, but do not let it boil.

7. Serve hot and enjoy the authentic taste of Clam Chowder.

KUMARA AND BACON SOUP

Ingredients:

- 500g bacon, diced

- 2 large kumara, peeled and chopped
- 1 large onion, chopped
- 3 cloves of garlic, minced
- 1 tsp paprika powder
- 6 cups of chicken broth
- 1 cup of heavy cream
- Salt and pepper to taste

Instructions:

1. In a large pot, heat some oil and sauté the bacon until crisp.

2. Remove the bacon from the pot and set aside, leaving the bacon grease in the pot.

3. Sauté the onion and garlic in the bacon grease until soft.

4. Add the kumara to the pot and cook for a few minutes until slightly browned.

5. Add the paprika, chicken broth, salt, and pepper to the pot.

6. Bring the mixture to a boil, then reduce the heat and let it simmer for 20-30 minutes or until the kumara is tender.

7. Stir in the heavy cream and heat until warm, but do not let it boil.

8. Serve hot and sprinkle the crispy bacon on top. Enjoy the authentic taste of Kumara and Bacon soup.

MUSSEL CHOWDER

Ingredients:

- 1 kg of mussels, cleaned and removed from the shells
- 2 large potatoes, peeled and chopped
- 1 large onion, chopped
- 3 cloves of garlic, minced
- 1 cup of corn kernels
- 1 tsp dried thyme
- 6 cups of fish broth
- 1 cup of heavy cream
- Salt and pepper to taste

Instructions:

1. In a large pot, heat some oil and sauté the onion and garlic until soft.

2. Add the potatoes to the pot and cook for a few minutes until slightly browned.

3. Add the corn, thyme, fish broth, salt, and pepper to the pot.

4. Bring the mixture to a boil, then reduce the heat and let it simmer for 20-30 minutes or until the potatoes are tender.

5. Add the mussels to the pot and cook for 5-7 minutes or until they have opened up and are fully cooked.

6. Stir in the heavy cream and heat until warm, but do not let it boil.
7. Serve hot and enjoy the authentic taste of Mussel Chowder.

PARSNIP AND KUMARA SOUP

Ingredients:

- 2 large parsnips, peeled and chopped
- 2 large kumara, peeled and chopped
- 1 large onion, chopped
- 3 cloves of garlic, minced
- 1 tsp dried thyme
- 6 cups of chicken broth
- 1 cup of heavy cream
- Salt and pepper to taste

Instructions:

1. In a large pot, heat some oil and sauté the onion and garlic until soft.

2. Add the parsnips and kumara to the pot and cook for a few minutes until slightly browned.

3. Add the thyme, chicken broth, salt, and pepper to the pot.

4. Bring the mixture to a boil, then reduce the heat and let it simmer for 20-30 minutes or until the vegetables are tender.

5. Use a blender or immersion blender to blend the mixture until smooth.

6. Stir in the heavy cream and heat until warm, but do not let it boil.

7. Serve hot and enjoy the authentic taste of Parsnip and Kumara soup.

STEWS

KUMARA STEW

Ingredients:

- 3 large kumara, peeled and chopped into small pieces
- 1 large onion, chopped
- 2 cloves of garlic, minced
- 1 red bell pepper, chopped
- 1 teaspoon of dried thyme
- 1 teaspoon of paprika
- 1 teaspoon of salt
- 1 teaspoon of black pepper
- 2 cups of vegetable broth
- 1 tablespoon of olive oil

Instructions:

1. Heat the olive oil in a large pot over medium heat. Add the chopped onion and garlic and cook until softened, about 5 minutes.

2. Add the chopped kumara, red bell pepper, thyme, paprika, salt, and black pepper to the pot. Stir to combine.

3. Pour in the vegetable broth and bring the mixture to a boil. Reduce heat to low and let the stew simmer for 20-25 minutes, or until the kumara is tender.

4. Serve the kumara stew hot, garnished with fresh herbs, if desired.

PORK AND KUMARA STEW

Ingredients:

- 1 lb of pork shoulder, cut into 1-inch pieces
- 3 large kumara, peeled and chopped into small pieces
- 1 large onion, chopped
- 2 cloves of garlic, minced
- 1 red bell pepper, chopped
- 1 teaspoon of dried thyme
- 1 teaspoon of paprika
- 1 teaspoon of salt
- 1 teaspoon of black pepper
- 2 cups of chicken broth
- 1 tablespoon of olive oil

Instructions:

1. Heat the olive oil in a large pot over medium heat. Add the chopped onion and garlic and cook until softened, about 5 minutes.

2. Add the pork pieces to the pot and cook until browned on all sides, about 5-7 minutes.

3. Add the chopped kumara, red bell pepper, thyme, paprika, salt, and black pepper to the pot. Stir to combine.

4. Pour in the chicken broth and bring the mixture to a boil. Reduce heat to low and let the stew simmer for 30-35 minutes, or until the pork is tender and the kumara is soft.

5. Serve the pork and kumara stew hot, garnished with fresh herbs, if desired.

CHICKEN AND KUMARA STEW

Ingredients:

- 1 lb of chicken breast, cut into 1-inch pieces
- 3 large kumara, peeled and chopped into small pieces
- 1 large onion, chopped
- 2 cloves of garlic, minced
- 1 red bell pepper, chopped
- 1 teaspoon of dried thyme
- 1 teaspoon of paprika
- 1 teaspoon of salt
- 1 teaspoon of black pepper
- 2 cups of chicken broth
- 1 tablespoon of olive oil

Instructions:

1. Heat the olive oil in a large pot over medium heat. Add the chopped onion and garlic and cook until softened, about 5 minutes.

2. Add the chicken pieces to the pot and cook until browned on all sides, about 5-7 minutes.

3. Add the chopped kumara, red bell pepper, thyme, paprika, salt, and black pepper to the pot. Stir to combine.

4. Pour in the chicken broth and bring the mixture to a boil. Reduce heat to low and let the stew simmer for 20-25 minutes, or until the chicken is cooked through and the kumara is soft.

5. Serve the chicken and kumara stew hot, garnished with fresh herbs, if desired.

MUTTON AND POTATO STEW

Ingredients:

- 1 lb of mutton, cut into 1-inch pieces
- 3 large potatoes, peeled and chopped into small pieces
- 1 large onion, chopped
- 2 cloves of garlic, minced
- 1 red bell pepper, chopped
- 1 teaspoon of dried thyme
- 1 teaspoon of paprika
- 1 teaspoon of salt
- 1 teaspoon of black pepper
- 2 cups of chicken broth
- 1 tablespoon of olive oil

Instructions:

1. Heat the olive oil in a large pot over medium heat. Add the chopped onion and garlic and cook until softened, about 5 minutes.

2. Add the mutton pieces to the pot and cook until browned on all sides, about 5-7 minutes.

3. Add the chopped potatoes, red bell pepper, thyme, paprika, salt, and black pepper to the pot. Stir to combine.

4. Pour in the chicken broth and bring the mixture to a boil. Reduce heat to low and let the stew simmer for 30-35 minutes.

5. Serve the mutton and potato stew hot, garnished with fresh herbs, if desired.

RĪWAI AND PORK STEW

Ingredients:

- 1 lb of pork shoulder, cut into 1-inch pieces
- 2 large rīwai, peeled and chopped into small pieces
- 1 large onion, chopped
- 2 cloves of garlic, minced
- 1 red bell pepper, chopped
- 1 teaspoon of dried thyme
- 1 teaspoon of paprika
- 1 teaspoon of salt
- 1 teaspoon of black pepper
- 2 cups of chicken broth
- 1 tablespoon of olive oil

Instructions:

1. Heat the olive oil in a large pot over medium heat. Add the chopped onion and garlic and cook until softened, about 5 minutes.

2. Add the pork pieces to the pot and cook until browned on all sides, about 5-7 minutes.

3. Add the chopped rīwai, red bell pepper, thyme, paprika, salt, and black pepper to the pot. Stir to combine.

4. Pour in the chicken broth and bring the mixture to a boil. Reduce heat to low and let the stew simmer for 30-35 minutes, or until the pork is tender and the rīwai is soft.

5. Serve the rīwai and pork stew hot, garnished with fresh herbs, if desired.

BEEF AND KUMARA STEW

Ingredients:

- 1 lb of beef, cut into 1-inch pieces
- 3 large kumara, peeled and chopped into small pieces
- 1 large onion, chopped
- 2 cloves of garlic, minced
- 1 red bell pepper, chopped
- 1 teaspoon of dried thyme
- 1 teaspoon of paprika
- 1 teaspoon of salt
- 1 teaspoon of black pepper
- 2 cups of beef broth
- 1 tablespoon of olive oil

Instructions:

1. Heat the olive oil in a large pot over medium heat. Add the chopped onion and garlic and cook until softened, about 5 minutes.

2. Add the beef pieces to the pot and cook until browned on all sides, about 5-7 minutes.

3. Add the chopped kumara, red bell pepper, thyme, paprika, salt, and black pepper to the pot. Stir to combine.

4. Pour in the beef broth and bring the mixture to a boil. Reduce heat to low and let the stew simmer for 30-35 minutes, or until the beef is tender and the kumara is soft.

5. Serve the beef and kumara stew hot, garnished with fresh herbs, if desired.

MUTTON AND KUMARA STEW

Ingredients:

- 1 lb of mutton, cut into 1-inch pieces
- 3 large kumara, peeled and chopped into small pieces
- 1 large onion, chopped
- 2 cloves of garlic, minced
- 1 red bell pepper, chopped
- 1 teaspoon of dried thyme
- 1 teaspoon of paprika
- 1 teaspoon of salt
- 1 teaspoon of black pepper
- 2 cups of chicken broth
- 1 tablespoon of olive oil

Instructions:

1. Heat the olive oil in a large pot over medium heat. Add the chopped onion and garlic and cook until softened, about 5 minutes.

2. Add the mutton pieces to the pot and cook until browned on all sides, about 5-7 minutes.

3. Add the chopped kumara, red bell pepper, thyme, paprika, salt, and black pepper to the pot. Stir to combine.

4. Pour in the chicken broth and bring the mixture to a boil. Reduce heat to low and let the stew simmer for 30-35 minutes, or until the mutton is tender and the kumara is soft.

5. Serve the mutton and kumara stew hot, garnished with fresh herbs, if desired.

RABBIT AND KUMARA STEW

Ingredients:

- 1 lb of rabbit, cut into 1-inch pieces
- 3 large kumara, peeled and chopped into small pieces
- 1 large onion, chopped
- 2 cloves of garlic, minced
- 1 red bell pepper, chopped
- 1 teaspoon of dried thyme
- 1 teaspoon of paprika
- 1 teaspoon of salt
- 1 teaspoon of black pepper
- 2 cups of chicken broth
- 1 tablespoon of olive oil

Instructions:

1. Heat the olive oil in a large pot over medium heat. Add the chopped onion and garlic and cook until softened, about 5 minutes.

2. Add the rabbit pieces to the pot and cook until browned on all sides.

3. Add the chopped kumara, red bell pepper, thyme, paprika, salt, and black pepper to the pot. Stir to combine.

4. Pour in the chicken broth and bring the mixture to a boil. Reduce heat to low and let the stew simmer for 30-35 minutes, or until the rabbit is tender and the kumara is soft.

5. Serve the rabbit and kumara stew hot, garnished with fresh herbs, if desired.

BEEF AND POTATO STEW

Ingredients:

- 1 lb of beef, cut into 1-inch pieces
- 3 large potatoes, peeled and chopped into small pieces
- 1 large onion, chopped
- 2 cloves of garlic, minced
- 1 red bell pepper, chopped
- 1 teaspoon of dried thyme
- 1 teaspoon of paprika
- 1 teaspoon of salt
- 1 teaspoon of black pepper
- 2 cups of beef broth
- 1 tablespoon of olive oil

Instructions:

1. Heat the olive oil in a large pot over medium heat. Add the chopped onion and garlic and cook until softened, about 5 minutes.

2. Add the beef pieces to the pot and cook until browned on all sides, about 5-7 minutes.

3. Add the chopped potatoes, red bell pepper, thyme, paprika, salt, and black pepper to the pot. Stir to combine.

4. Pour in the beef broth and bring the mixture to a boil. Reduce heat to low and let the stew simmer for 30-35 minutes, or until the beef is tender and the potatoes are soft.

5. Serve the beef and potato stew hot, garnished with fresh herbs, if desired.

VENISON AND KUMARA STEW

Ingredients:

- 1 lb of venison, cut into 1-inch pieces
- 3 large kumara, peeled and chopped into small pieces
- 1 large onion, chopped
- 2 cloves of garlic, minced
- 1 red bell pepper, chopped
- 1 teaspoon of dried thyme
- 1 teaspoon of paprika
- 1 teaspoon of salt
- 1 teaspoon of black pepper
- 2 cups of beef broth
- 1 tablespoon of olive oil

Instructions:

1. Heat the olive oil in a large pot over medium heat. Add the chopped onion and garlic and cook until softened.

2. Add the venison pieces to the pot and cook until browned on all sides, about 5-7 minutes.

3. Add the chopped kumara, red bell pepper, thyme, paprika, salt, and black pepper to the pot. Stir to combine.

4. Pour in the beef broth and bring the mixture to a boil. Reduce heat to low and let the stew simmer for 30-35 minutes, or until the venison is tender and the kumara is soft.

5. Serve the venison and kumara stew hot, garnished with fresh herbs, if desired.

SEAFOOD

FRIED TĪTĪ (MUTTONBIRD)

Ingredients:

- 500g Tītī (Muttonbird) fillets
- 1 cup flour
- 1 teaspoon salt
- 1 teaspoon black pepper
- 1 teaspoon paprika
- 1/2 teaspoon garlic powder
- 1/2 teaspoon onion powder
- 1/2 teaspoon dried thyme
- 1 cup oil for frying

Instructions:

1. Cut Tītī fillets into smaller pieces.

2. In a bowl, mix together the flour, salt, black pepper, paprika, garlic powder, onion powder, and dried thyme.

3. Coat each Tītī piece in the flour mixture.

4. Heat the oil in a large pan over medium heat.

5. Fry the Tītī pieces until golden brown on both sides, about 5 minutes per side.

6. Remove from the pan and drain on paper towels.

7. Serve hot with your favorite dipping sauce.

HĀPUKA AND KUMARA BAKE

Ingredients:

- 1 Hāpuka fillet
- 2 medium kumara, peeled and diced
- 1 onion, diced
- 2 cloves garlic, minced
- 1/4 cup white wine
- 1/4 cup chicken stock
- 1 tablespoon olive oil
- 1 teaspoon salt
- 1/2 teaspoon black pepper
- 1/4 teaspoon dried thyme
- 1/4 teaspoon paprika

Instructions:

1. Preheat the oven to 200°C.

2. In a large oven-proof dish, place the Hāpuka fillet in the center.

3. Surround the Hāpuka fillet with the diced kumara, onion, and minced garlic.

4. Drizzle the olive oil over the Hāpuka and vegetables.

5. In a small bowl, mix together the white wine, chicken stock, salt, black pepper, dried thyme, and paprika.

6. Pour the mixture over the Hāpuka and vegetables.

7. Cover the dish with foil and bake in the oven for 25 minutes.

8. Remove the foil and bake for an additional 10 minutes, or until the Hāpuka is cooked through and the kumara is tender.

9. Serve hot.

STEAMED MUSSELS

Ingredients:

- 2 pounds fresh mussels, scrubbed and debearded
- 2 tablespoons butter
- 1 onion, diced
- 2 cloves garlic, minced
- 1/2 cup white wine
- 1/2 cup chicken stock
- 1 teaspoon salt
- 1/2 teaspoon black pepper
- 1/4 teaspoon dried thyme
- 1/4 teaspoon paprika

Instructions:

1. In a large pot, heat the butter over medium heat.

2. Add the diced onion and minced garlic to the pot and cook until softened, about 5 minutes.

3. Add the white wine, chicken stock, salt, black pepper, dried thyme, and paprika to the pot and bring to a boil.

4. Add the mussels to the pot and cover with a lid.

5. Steam the mussels for 5-7 minutes, or until they have opened.

6. Discard any mussels that do not open.

7. Serve the mussels in a large bowl with the broth.

GRILLED SQUID

Ingredients:

- 1 pound fresh squid, cleaned and cut into rings
- 1/4 cup olive oil
- 1 teaspoon salt
- 1/2 teaspoon black pepper
- 1/4 teaspoon paprika
- 1 lemon, cut into wedges

Instructions:

1. In a large bowl, mix together the olive oil, salt, black pepper, and paprika.

2. Add the squid rings to the bowl and toss to coat in the marinade.

3. Preheat a grill to high heat.

4. Lightly oil the grill grates.

5. Grill the squid rings for 2-3 minutes on each side, or until they are charred and cooked through.

6. Serve the grilled squid with lemon wedges on the side.

POACHED SALMON

Ingredients:

- 2 pounds salmon fillet
- 1 onion, sliced
- 2 carrots, sliced

- 2 stalks celery, sliced
- 2 cloves garlic, minced
- 1 bay leaf
- 1 teaspoon salt
- 1/2 teaspoon black pepper
- 1/4 teaspoon dried thyme
- 4 cups water
- 1/4 cup white wine

Instructions:

1. In a large pot, place the salmon fillet, onion, carrots, celery, garlic, bay leaf, salt, black pepper, dried thyme, water, and white wine.

2. Bring the mixture to a boil over high heat, then reduce the heat to low.

3. Simmer the salmon for 10-12 minutes, or until it is cooked through.

4. Remove the salmon from the pot and place it on a serving platter.

5. Serve the poached salmon hot, garnished with freshly chopped herbs if desired.

LOBSTER TAILS IN BUTTER SAUCE

Ingredients:

- 4 lobster tails
- 1/2 cup butter
- 2 cloves garlic, minced
- 1/4 cup white wine
- 1/4 cup chicken stock
- 1 teaspoon salt

- 1/2 teaspoon black pepper
- 1/4 teaspoon dried thyme
- 1/4 teaspoon paprika

Instructions:

1. Preheat a grill to high heat.

2. Cut the lobster tails in half lengthwise.

3. In a small saucepan, melt the butter over medium heat.

4. Add the minced garlic to the saucepan and cook for 1 minute.

5. Add the white wine, chicken stock, salt, black pepper, dried thyme, and paprika to the saucepan and stir to combine.

6. Brush the lobster tails with the butter sauce.

7. Grill the lobster tails for 5-7 minutes on each side, or until they are cooked through and the shells are bright red.

8. Serve the lobster tails hot with additional butter sauce on the side.

FRIED SNAPPER

Ingredients:

- 2 pounds snapper fillets
- 1 cup flour
- 1 teaspoon salt
- 1 teaspoon black pepper

- 1 teaspoon paprika
- 1/2 teaspoon garlic powder
- 1/2 teaspoon onion powder
- 1/2 teaspoon dried thyme
- 1 cup oil for frying

Instructions:

1. Cut the snapper fillets into smaller pieces.

2. In a bowl, mix together the flour, salt, black pepper, paprika, garlic powder, onion powder, and dried thyme.

3. Coat each snapper piece in the flour mixture.

4. Heat the oil in a large pan over medium heat.

5. Fry the snapper pieces until golden brown on both sides, about 5 minutes per side.

6. Remove from the pan and drain on paper towels.

7. Serve hot with your favorite dipping sauce.

TUNA STEAKS WITH LEMON BUTTER

Ingredients:

- 4 tuna steaks
- 1/4 cup butter
- 2 cloves garlic, minced
- 1 lemon, juiced
- 1 teaspoon salt
- 1/2 teaspoon black pepper
- 1/4 teaspoon dried thyme

Instructions:

1. In a small saucepan, melt the butter over medium heat.

2. Add the minced garlic to the saucepan and cook for 1 minute.

3. Stir in the lemon juice, salt, black pepper, and dried thyme to the saucepan.

4. Preheat a grill to high heat.

5. Brush the tuna steaks with the lemon butter sauce.

6. Grill the tuna steaks for 4-5 minutes on each side, or until they are cooked to your desired level of doneness.

7. Serve the tuna steaks hot with additional lemon butter sauce on the side.

GRILLED SCALLOPS

Ingredients:

- 1 pound fresh scallops
- 1/4 cup olive oil
- 1 teaspoon salt
- 1/2 teaspoon black pepper
- 1/4 teaspoon paprika
- 1 lemon, cut into wedges

Instructions:

1. In a large bowl, mix together the olive oil, salt, black pepper, and paprika.

2. Add the scallops to the bowl and toss to coat in the marinade.

3. Preheat a grill to high heat. Lightly oil the grill grates.

4. Grill the scallops for 2-3 minutes on each side, or until they are charred and cooked through.

5. Serve the grilled scallops with lemon wedges on the side.

FRIED PĀUA

Ingredients:

- 1 pound pāua, cleaned and sliced
- 1 cup flour
- 1 teaspoon salt
- 1/2 teaspoon black pepper
- 1/4 teaspoon paprika
- 1/2 teaspoon garlic powder
- 1/2 teaspoon onion powder
- 1/2 teaspoon dried thyme
- 1 cup oil for frying

Instructions:

1. In a bowl, mix together the flour, salt, black pepper, paprika, garlic powder, onion powder, and dried thyme.

2. Coat each pāua slice in the flour mixture.

3. Heat the oil in a large pan over medium heat.

4. Fry the pāua slices until golden brown on both sides, about 5 minutes per side.

5. Remove from the pan and drain on paper towels.

6. Serve hot with your favorite dipping sauce.

LAMB

ROASTED LEG OF LAMB

Ingredients:

- 1 (6-7 pound) leg of lamb
- 2 teaspoons salt
- 1 teaspoon black pepper
- 1 teaspoon dried rosemary
- 1 teaspoon dried thyme
- 3 cloves garlic, minced
- 1/4 cup olive oil

Instructions:

1. Preheat oven to 450°F.

2. In a small bowl, mix together salt, pepper, rosemary, thyme, garlic, and olive oil.

3. Place the leg of lamb in a roasting pan and rub the herb mixture all over the lamb.

4. Roast for 15 minutes, then reduce the heat to 350°F and continue roasting for another hour, or until the internal temperature of the lamb reaches 145°F.

5. Let the lamb rest for 10-15 minutes before carving and serving.

FRIED LAMB CHOPS

Ingredients:

- 4 lamb chops
- 1 cup flour
- 2 teaspoons salt
- 1 teaspoon black pepper
- 1 teaspoon paprika
- 1 teaspoon garlic powder
- 1/2 teaspoon onion powder
- 1 egg
- 1/2 cup milk
- Vegetable oil for frying

Instructions:

1. In a shallow dish, mix together flour, salt, pepper, paprika, garlic powder, and onion powder.

2. In a separate shallow dish, beat together egg and milk.

3. Dip each lamb chop in the flour mixture, then in the egg mixture, and then back in the flour mixture.

4. Heat about 1 inch of oil in a large heavy skillet over medium-high heat.

5. Fry the lamb chops for 3-4 minutes on each side, or until golden brown.

6. Drain on paper towels and serve hot.

BRAISED LAMB SHANK

Ingredients:

- 4 lamb shanks
- 2 teaspoons salt
- 1 teaspoon black pepper
- 1 tablespoon olive oil
- 1 onion, chopped
- 3 cloves garlic, minced
- 1 cup red wine
- 1 cup beef broth
- 2 tablespoons tomato paste
- 1 teaspoon dried thyme
- 1 teaspoon dried rosemary
- 2 carrots, chopped
- 2 celery stalks, chopped

Instructions:

1. Season the lamb shanks with salt and pepper.

2. In a large Dutch oven or heavy pot, heat the olive oil over medium-high heat.

3. Brown the lamb shanks on all sides, about 5 minutes per side.

4. Remove the lamb shanks from the pot and set aside.

5. Add the onion, garlic, carrots, and celery to the pot and cook until the vegetables are soft, about 5 minutes.

6. Stir in the red wine, beef broth, tomato paste, thyme, and rosemary.

7. Return the lamb shanks to the pot, making sure they are submerged in the liquid.

8. Bring the mixture to a boil, then reduce heat to low, cover, and simmer for 2-3 hours, or until the lamb is tender and falling off the bone.

9. Serve hot with the braising liquid and vegetables.

LAMB CURRY

Ingredients:

- 1 pound boneless lamb, cut into bite-sized pieces
- 2 tablespoons vegetable oil
- 1 onion, chopped
- 3 cloves garlic, minced
- 1 tablespoon grated ginger
- 2 teaspoons ground coriander
- 1 teaspoon ground cumin
- 1 teaspoon turmeric
- 1/2 teaspoon cayenne pepper
- 1 can (14.5 ounces) diced tomatoes
- 1 cup chicken broth
- 1 cup coconut milk
- Salt and pepper to taste

Instructions:

1. In a large pot or Dutch oven, heat the oil over medium-high heat.

2. Add the onion, garlic, and ginger and cook until the onion is soft, about 5 minutes.

3. Add the lamb and cook until browned on all sides, about 5 minutes.

4. Stir in the coriander, cumin, turmeric, and cayenne pepper.

5. Add the diced tomatoes, chicken broth, and coconut milk.

6. Bring the mixture to a boil, then reduce heat to low, cover, and simmer for 1-2 hours, or until the lamb is tender.

7. Season with salt and pepper to taste.

8. Serve hot with rice or naan bread.

LAMB AND KUMARA STEW

Ingredients:

- 1 pound boneless lamb, cut into bite-sized pieces
- 2 tablespoons olive oil
- 1 onion, chopped
- 3 cloves garlic, minced
- 2 cups chicken broth
- 2 cups diced kumara (sweet potato)
- 1 cup diced carrots
- 1 cup diced celery
- 1 teaspoon dried thyme
- 1 teaspoon dried rosemary
- Salt and pepper to taste

Instructions:

1. In a large pot or Dutch oven, heat the olive oil over medium-high heat.

2. Add the onion and garlic and cook until the onion is soft, about 5 minutes.

3. Add the lamb and cook until browned on all sides, about 5 minutes.

4. Stir in the chicken broth, kumara, carrots, celery, thyme, and rosemary.

5. Bring the mixture to a boil, then reduce heat to low, cover, and simmer for 1-2 hours, or until the lamb and vegetables are tender.

6. Season with salt and pepper to taste.

7. Serve hot with crusty bread or over rice.

LAMB AND POTATO PIE

Ingredients:

- 1 pound boneless lamb, cut into bite-sized pieces
- 2 tablespoons butter
- 1 onion, chopped
- 3 cloves garlic, minced
- 2 cups chicken broth
- 2 cups diced potatoes
- 1 cup frozen peas
- 1 teaspoon dried thyme
- 1 teaspoon dried rosemary
- Salt and pepper to taste
- 1 refrigerated pie crust
- 1 egg, beaten

Instructions:

1. Preheat oven to 425°F.

2. In a large pot or Dutch oven, melt the butter over medium-high heat.

3. Add the onion and garlic and cook until the onion is soft, about 5 minutes.

4. Add the lamb and cook until browned on all sides, about 5 minutes.

5. Stir in the chicken broth, potatoes, peas, thyme, and rosemary.

6. Bring the mixture to a boil, then reduce heat to low, cover, and simmer for 20-30 minutes, or until the potatoes are tender.

7. Season with salt and pepper to taste.

8. Roll out one pie crust and place it in a 9-inch pie dish.

9. Pour the lamb and potato mixture into the pie dish.

10. Roll out the second pie crust and place it on top of the filling.

11. Cut several slits in the top crust to allow steam to escape.

12. Brush the top crust with beaten egg.

13. Bake for 25-30 minutes, or until the crust is golden brown.

14. Serve hot.

GRILLED LAMB CUTLETS

Ingredients:

- 8 lamb cutlets
- 2 teaspoons salt
- 1 teaspoon black pepper
- 2 cloves garlic, minced
- 1/4 cup olive oil
- 1 lemon, juiced

Instructions:

1. In a small bowl, mix together salt, pepper, garlic, olive oil, and lemon juice.

2. Place the lamb cutlets in a shallow dish and pour the marinade over the lamb.

3. Cover and refrigerate for 1 hour, or up to overnight.

4. Preheat grill to high heat.

5. Remove the lamb cutlets from the marinade and discard the marinade.

6. Place the lamb cutlets on the grill and cook for 2-3 minutes on each side, or until the internal temperature reaches 145°F.

7. Serve hot with lemon wedges.

FRIED LAMB STEAKS

Ingredients:

- 4 lamb steaks
- 1 cup flour
- 2 teaspoons salt
- 1 teaspoon black pepper
- 1 teaspoon paprika
- 1 teaspoon garlic powder
- 1/2 teaspoon onion powder
- 1 egg
- 1/2 cup milk
- Vegetable oil for frying

Instructions:

1. In a shallow dish, mix together flour, salt, pepper, paprika, garlic powder, and onion powder.

2. In a separate shallow dish, beat together egg and milk.

3. Dip each lamb steak in the flour mixture, then in the egg mixture, then back in the flour mixture.

4. In a large heavy skillet, heat the vegetable oil over medium-high heat.

5. Fry the lamb steaks for 3-4 minutes on each side, or until golden brown and crispy.

6. Drain on paper towels.

7. Serve hot with your favorite dipping sauce.

LAMB AND PUMPKIN CASSEROLE

Ingredients:

- 1 pound boneless lamb, cut into bite-sized pieces
- 2 tablespoons butter
- 1 onion, chopped
- 3 cloves garlic, minced
- 2 cups chicken broth
- 2 cups diced pumpkin
- 1 teaspoon dried thyme
- 1 teaspoon dried rosemary
- Salt and pepper to taste
- 1 cup breadcrumbs
- 1/4 cup grated Parmesan cheese

Instructions:

1. Preheat oven to 375°F.

2. In a large pot or Dutch oven, melt the butter over medium-high heat.

3. Add the onion and garlic and cook until the onion is soft, about 5 minutes.

4. Add the lamb and cook until browned on all sides, about 5 minutes.

5. Stir in the chicken broth, pumpkin, thyme, and rosemary.

6. Bring the mixture to a boil, then reduce heat to low, cover, and simmer for 20-30 minutes, or until the pumpkin is tender.

7. Season with salt and pepper to taste.

8. Transfer the lamb and pumpkin mixture to a 9x13 inch baking dish.

9. In a small bowl, mix together breadcrumbs and Parmesan cheese.

10. Sprinkle the breadcrumb mixture over the top of the casserole.

11. Bake for 20-25 minutes, or until the breadcrumbs are golden brown.

12. Serve hot.

LAMB AND CARROT STEW

Ingredients:

- 1 pound boneless lamb, cut into bite-sized pieces
- 2 tablespoons olive oil
- 1 onion, chopped
- 3 cloves garlic, minced
- 2 cups chicken broth
- 2 cups diced carrots
- 1 teaspoon dried thyme
- 1 teaspoon dried rosemary
- Salt and pepper to taste

Instructions:

1. In a large pot or Dutch oven, heat the olive oil over medium-high heat.

2. Add the onion and garlic and cook until the onion is soft, about 5 minutes.

3. Add the lamb and cook until browned on all sides, about 5 minutes.

4. Stir in the chicken broth, carrots, thyme, and rosemary.

5. Bring the mixture to a boil, then reduce heat to low, cover, and simmer for 1-2 hours, or until the lamb and carrots are tender.

6. Season with salt and pepper to taste.

7. Serve hot with crusty bread or over rice.

PORK

ROASTED PORK BELLY

Ingredients:

- 1 kg pork belly
- 3 cloves of garlic, minced
- 1 tbsp salt
- 1 tsp black pepper
- 2 tbsp olive oil

Instructions:

1. Preheat the oven to 200°C.

2. In a small bowl, mix together the minced garlic, salt, black pepper, and olive oil.

3. Rub the mixture over the pork belly.

4. Place the pork belly on a roasting pan and roast in the oven for 30 minutes.

5. Reduce the oven temperature to 180°C and continue roasting for another hour.

6. Take the pork belly out of the oven and let it rest for 10 minutes before slicing and serving.

FRIED PORK CHOPS

Ingredients:

- 4 pork chops
- 1 cup flour
- 1 tsp salt
- 1 tsp black pepper
- 2 eggs, beaten
- 1 cup breadcrumbs
- 1/4 cup vegetable oil

Instructions:

1. In a shallow dish, mix together the flour, salt, and black pepper.

2. In another shallow dish, beat the eggs.

3. In a third shallow dish, place the breadcrumbs.

4. Dip each pork chop into the flour mixture, then into the beaten eggs, and finally into the breadcrumbs.

5. Heat the vegetable oil in a large frying pan over medium heat.

6. Fry the pork chops for 3-4 minutes on each side, or until golden brown and cooked through.

7. Remove from the pan and let it rest for a few minutes before serving.

BRAISED PORK SHOULDER

Ingredients:

- 1 kg pork shoulder
- 3 cloves of garlic, minced
- 1 onion, diced
- 2 carrots, diced
- 2 stalks of celery, diced
- 1 cup chicken broth
- 1 cup red wine
- 2 tbsp olive oil
- 1 tsp salt
- 1 tsp black pepper

Instructions:

1. In a large pot, heat the olive oil over medium heat.

2. Add the minced garlic, onion, carrots, and celery and cook until the vegetables are soft and fragrant.

3. Add the pork shoulder to the pot and brown on all sides.

4. Pour in the chicken broth and red wine. Bring the mixture to a boil.

5. Reduce the heat to low, cover the pot, and let it simmer for 2-3 hours, or until the pork is tender and falling apart.

6. Remove the pork from the pot and let it rest for 10 minutes before shredding with a fork.

7. Serve the braised pork with the vegetables and sauce.

PORK CURRY

Ingredients:

- 1 kg pork, cut into bite-sized pieces
- 2 onions, diced
- 3 cloves of garlic, minced
- 2 tbsp curry powder
- 1 tsp turmeric
- 1 tsp cumin
- 1 tsp coriander
- 1 can of coconut milk
- 1 tbsp olive oil
- 1 tsp salt
- 1 tsp black pepper

Instructions:

1. In a large pot, heat the olive oil over medium heat.

2. Add the diced onions and minced garlic and cook until the vegetables are soft and fragrant.

3. Add the curry powder, turmeric, cumin, and coriander to the pot and cook for another minute.

4. Add the pork to the pot and cook until browned on all sides.

5. Pour in the can of coconut milk and bring the mixture to a boil.

6. Reduce the heat to low and let it simmer for 30-40 minutes, or until the pork is cooked through and the sauce has thickened.

7. Season with salt and black pepper to taste.

8. Serve the pork curry over rice.

PORK AND KUMARA STEW

Ingredients:

- 1 kg pork, cut into bite-sized pieces
- 2 large kumara, peeled and diced
- 2 onions, diced
- 3 cloves of garlic, minced
- 1 cup chicken broth
- 1 cup red wine
- 2 tbsp olive oil
- 1 tsp salt
- 1 tsp black pepper

Instructions:

1. In a large pot, heat the olive oil over medium heat.

2. Add the diced onions and minced garlic and cook until the vegetables are soft and fragrant.

3. Add the pork to the pot and cook until browned on all sides.

4. Add the diced kumara to the pot.

5. Pour in the chicken broth and red wine. Bring the mixture to a boil.

6. Reduce the heat to low, cover the pot, and let it simmer for 30-40 minutes, or until the pork and kumara are cooked through and tender.

7. Season with salt and black pepper to taste.

8. Serve the pork and kumara stew hot.

PORK AND POTATO PIE

Ingredients:

- 1 kg pork, cooked and shredded
- 3 large potatoes, peeled and sliced
- 1 onion, diced
- 2 cloves of garlic, minced
- 1 cup chicken broth
- 1 tsp salt
- 1 tsp black pepper
- 1 tbsp olive oil
- 1 sheet of puff pastry, thawed

Instructions:

1. Preheat the oven to 200°C.

2. In a large pot, heat the olive oil over medium heat.

3. Add the diced onion and minced garlic and cook until the vegetables are soft and fragrant.

4. Add the sliced potatoes to the pot and cook for 5 minutes, stirring occasionally.

5. Pour in the chicken broth and bring the mixture to a boil.

6. Reduce the heat to low and let it simmer for 10-15 minutes, or until the potatoes are tender.

7. In a large bowl, mix together the cooked and shredded pork, the potato mixture, salt, and black pepper.

8. Roll out the puff pastry on a lightly floured surface.

9. Spoon the pork and potato mixture into a 9-inch pie dish.

10. Place the puff pastry over the top of the pie dish, trimming any excess pastry.

11. Bake the pork and potato pie in the oven for 20-25 minutes, or until the pastry is golden brown and puffed.

12. Let the pie cool for 10 minutes before serving.

GRILLED PORK TENDERLOIN

Ingredients:

- 2 pork tenderloins
- 3 cloves of garlic, minced
- 1 tbsp olive oil
- 1 tsp salt
- 1 tsp black pepper

Instructions:

1. In a small bowl, mix together the minced garlic, olive oil, salt, and black pepper.

2. Rub the mixture over the pork tenderloins.

3. Heat a grill or grill pan over medium-high heat.

4. Place the pork tenderloins on the grill and cook for 4-5 minutes on each side, or until the internal temperature reaches 145°F.

5. Remove the pork tenderloins from the grill and let it rest for 5 minutes before slicing and serving.

FRIED PORK STEAKS

Ingredients:

- 4 pork steaks
- 1 cup flour
- 1 tsp salt
- 1 tsp black pepper
- 2 eggs, beaten
- 1 cup breadcrumbs
- 1/4 cup vegetable oil

Instructions:

1. In a shallow dish, mix together the flour, salt, and black pepper.

2. In another shallow dish, beat the eggs.

3. In a third shallow dish, place the breadcrumbs.

4. Dip each pork steak into the flour mixture, then into the beaten eggs, and finally into the breadcrumbs.

5. Heat the vegetable oil in a large frying pan over medium heat.

6. Fry the pork steaks for 3-4 minutes on each side, or until golden brown and cooked through.

7. Remove from the pan and let it rest for a few minutes before serving.

PORK AND PUMPKIN CASSEROLE

Ingredients:

- 1 kg pork, cooked and shredded
- 1 large pumpkin, peeled and diced
- 2 onions, diced
- 3 cloves of garlic, minced
- 1 cup chicken broth
- 1 tsp salt
- 1 tsp black pepper
- 1 tbsp olive oil

Instructions:

1. Preheat the oven to 200°C.

2. In a large pot, heat the olive oil over medium heat.

3. Add the diced onions and minced garlic and cook until the vegetables are soft and fragrant.

4. Add the diced pumpkin to the pot and cook for 5 minutes, stirring occasionally.

5. Pour in the chicken broth and bring the mixture to a boil.

6. Reduce the heat to low and let it simmer for 10-15 minutes, or until the pumpkin is tender.

7. In a large bowl, mix together the cooked and shredded pork, the pumpkin mixture, salt, and black pepper.

8. Spoon the pork and pumpkin mixture into a 9x13 inch casserole dish.

9. Bake the casserole in the oven for 20-25 minutes, or until heated through.

10. Let the casserole cool for 10 minutes before serving.

PORK AND CARROT STEW

Ingredients:

- 1 kg pork, cut into bite-sized pieces
- 3 large carrots, peeled and diced
- 2 onions, diced
- 3 cloves of garlic, minced
- 1 cup chicken broth
- 1 cup red wine
- 2 tbsp olive oil
- 1 tsp salt
- 1 tsp black pepper

Instructions:

1. In a large pot, heat the olive oil over medium heat.

2. Add the diced onions and minced garlic and cook until the vegetables are soft and fragrant.

3. Add the pork to the pot and cook until browned on all sides.

4. Add the diced carrots to the pot.

5. Pour in the chicken broth and red wine. Bring the mixture to a boil.

6. Reduce the heat to low, cover the pot, and let it simmer for 30-40 minutes, or until the pork and carrots are cooked through and tender.

7. Season with salt and black pepper to taste.

8. Serve the pork and carrot stew hot.

POULTRY

ROASTED CHICKEN

Ingredients:

- 4 lbs chicken
- 2 tbsp olive oil
- 2 tsp salt
- 1 tsp black pepper
- 2 cloves of garlic, minced
- 1 lemon, sliced
- 1 sprig of rosemary

Instructions:

1. Preheat the oven to 425°F.

2. Rinse the chicken and pat it dry with paper towels.

3. In a bowl, mix together the olive oil, salt, pepper, and minced garlic.

4. Place the chicken in a roasting pan and rub the oil mixture all over it.

5. Arrange the lemon slices and rosemary sprig around the chicken.

6. Roast the chicken for about 45-50 minutes, or until the internal temperature reaches 165°F.

7. Let the chicken rest for 10 minutes before carving and serving.

FRIED CHICKEN WINGS

Ingredients:

- 2 lbs chicken wings
- 1 cup all-purpose flour
- 2 tsp salt
- 1 tsp black pepper
- 1 tsp paprika
- 1 tsp garlic powder
- 1 tsp onion powder
- 1 cup vegetable oil

Instructions:

1. In a bowl, mix together the flour, salt, pepper, paprika, garlic powder, and onion powder.

2. Dredge the chicken wings in the flour mixture, shaking off any excess.

3. Heat the oil in a large pan over medium-high heat.

4. Fry the chicken wings in batches for about 10 minutes, or until golden brown and cooked through.

5. Remove the chicken wings from the pan and drain on paper towels.

6. Serve the chicken wings hot with your favorite dipping sauce.

BRAISED CHICKEN THIGHS

Ingredients:

- 6 boneless, skinless chicken thighs
- 2 tbsp olive oil
- 2 onions, chopped
- 3 cloves of garlic, minced
- 1 cup chicken broth
- 1 can diced tomatoes
- 2 tbsp tomato paste
- 1 tsp salt
- 1 tsp black pepper
- 1 tsp dried thyme
- 1 tsp dried rosemary
- 1 tsp dried basil

Instructions:

1. In a large pan, heat the olive oil over medium heat.

2. Add the onions and garlic and cook until softened, about 5 minutes.

3. Add the chicken broth, diced tomatoes, tomato paste, salt, pepper, thyme, rosemary, and basil to the pan.

4. Stir to combine and bring the mixture to a boil.

5. Add the chicken thighs to the pan and cover with a lid.

6. Reduce the heat to low and simmer for about 30 minutes, or until the chicken is cooked through and tender.

7. Serve the chicken and sauce over rice or with crusty bread.

CHICKEN CURRY

Ingredients:

- 2 lbs boneless, skinless chicken, cut into bite-sized pieces
- 2 tbsp vegetable oil
- 1 onion, chopped
- 2 cloves of garlic, minced
- 1 tbsp ginger, grated
- 2 tbsp curry powder
- 1 tsp turmeric
- 1 tsp cumin
- 1 tsp coriander
- 1 can coconut milk
- 1 cup chicken broth
- 1 tsp salt
- 1 tsp black pepper

Instructions:

1. In a large pan, heat the vegetable oil over medium heat.

2. Add the onion, garlic, and ginger and cook until softened, about 5 minutes.

3. Add the curry powder, turmeric, cumin, and coriander to the pan and cook for 1-2 minutes, or until fragrant.

4. Add the chicken to the pan and cook until browned, about 5 minutes.

5. Stir in the coconut milk, chicken broth, salt, and pepper.

6. Bring the mixture to a boil and then reduce the heat to low.

7. Simmer for about 20-25 minutes, or until the chicken is cooked through and the sauce has thickened.

8. Serve the chicken curry with rice and garnish with cilantro, if desired.

CHICKEN AND KUMARA STEW

Ingredients:

- 2 lbs boneless, skinless chicken, cut into bite-sized pieces
- 2 tbsp olive oil
- 1 onion, chopped
- 2 cloves of garlic, minced
- 2 lbs kumara, peeled and diced
- 1 cup chicken broth
- 1 can diced tomatoes
- 1 tsp salt
- 1 tsp black pepper
- 1 tsp dried thyme
- 1 tsp dried rosemary
- 1 tsp dried basil

Instructions:

1. In a large pan, heat the olive oil over medium heat.

2. Add the onion and garlic and cook until softened, about 5 minutes.

3. Add the chicken and kumara to the pan and cook until the chicken is browned, about 5 minutes.

4. Stir in the chicken broth, diced tomatoes, salt, pepper, thyme, rosemary, and basil.

5. Bring the mixture to a boil and then reduce the heat to low.

6. Cover the pan with a lid and simmer for about 20-25 minutes, or until the chicken is cooked through and the kumara is tender.

7. Serve the chicken and kumara stew with crusty bread.

CHICKEN AND POTATO PIE

Ingredients:

- 2 lbs boneless, skinless chicken, cooked and shredded
- 2 lbs potatoes, peeled and sliced
- 1 onion, chopped
- 2 cloves of garlic, minced
- 1 cup chicken broth
- 1 cup heavy cream
- 1 tsp salt
- 1 tsp black pepper
- 1 tsp dried thyme
- 1 tsp dried rosemary
- 1/2 cup grated cheddar cheese
- 1 pie crust, store-bought or homemade

Instructions:

1. Preheat the oven to 375°F.

2. In a large pan, cook the potatoes in boiling water until tender, about 10 minutes. Drain and set aside.

3. In the same pan, heat a bit of oil over medium heat. Add the onion and garlic and cook until softened, about 5 minutes.

4. Stir in the chicken broth, heavy cream, salt, pepper, thyme, rosemary, and cheddar cheese.

5. Stir in the cooked chicken and potatoes and mix until combined.

6. Pour the mixture into a 9-inch pie dish and top with the pie crust.

7. Bake the pie for about 30-35 minutes, or until the crust is golden brown and the filling is hot and bubbly.

8. Let the pie cool for a few minutes before slicing and serving.

GRILLED CHICKEN BREASTS

Ingredients:

- 4 boneless, skinless chicken breasts
- 2 tbsp olive oil
- 2 tsp salt
- 1 tsp black pepper
- 1 tsp paprika
- 1 tsp garlic powder
- 1 tsp onion powder

Instructions:

1. Preheat the grill to medium-high heat.

2. In a bowl, mix together the olive oil, salt, pepper, paprika, garlic powder, and onion powder.

3. Brush the chicken breasts with the oil mixture and season both sides.

4. Place the chicken breasts on the grill and cook for 6-7 minutes on each side, or until the internal temperature reaches 165°F.

5. Remove the chicken from the grill and let it rest for a few minutes before slicing and serving.

FRIED CHICKEN DRUMSTICKS

Ingredients:

- 8 chicken drumsticks
- 1 cup all-purpose flour
- 2 tsp salt
- 1 tsp black pepper
- 1 tsp paprika
- 1 tsp garlic powder
- 1 tsp onion powder
- 1 cup vegetable oil

Instructions:

1. In a bowl, mix together the flour, salt, pepper, paprika, garlic powder, and onion powder.

2. Dredge the chicken drumsticks in the flour mixture, shaking off any excess.

3. Heat the oil in a large pan over medium-high heat.

4. Fry the chicken drumsticks in batches for about 10 minutes, or until golden brown and cooked through.

5. Remove the chicken drumsticks from the pan and drain on paper towels.

6. Serve the chicken drumsticks hot with your favorite dipping sauce.

CHICKEN AND PUMPKIN CASSEROLE

Ingredients:

- 2 lbs boneless, skinless chicken, cooked and shredded
- 2 lbs pumpkin, peeled and diced
- 1 onion, chopped
- 2 cloves of garlic, minced
- 1 cup chicken broth
- 1 cup heavy cream
- 1 tsp salt
- 1 tsp black pepper
- 1 tsp dried thyme
- 1 tsp dried rosemary
- 1/2 cup grated cheddar cheese
- 1 cup breadcrumbs
- 2 tbsp melted butter

Instructions:

1. Preheat the oven to 375°F.

2. In a large pan, cook the pumpkin in boiling water until tender, about 10 minutes. Drain and set aside.

3. In the same pan, heat a bit of oil over medium heat. Add the onion and garlic and cook until softened, about 5 minutes.

4. Stir in the chicken broth, heavy cream, salt, pepper, thyme, rosemary, and cheddar cheese.

5. Stir in the cooked chicken and pumpkin and mix until combined.

6. Pour the mixture into a 9x13 inch baking dish.

7. In a small bowl, mix together the breadcrumbs and melted butter. Sprinkle the mixture over the casserole.

8. Bake the casserole for about 25-30 minutes, or until the topping is golden brown and the filling is hot and bubbly.

9. Let the casserole cool for a few minutes before serving.

CHICKEN AND CARROT STEW

Ingredients:

- 2 lbs boneless, skinless chicken, cut into bite-sized pieces
- 2 tbsp olive oil
- 1 onion, chopped
- 2 cloves of garlic, minced
- 2 lbs carrots, peeled and diced
- 1 cup chicken broth
- 1 can diced tomatoes
- 1 tsp salt
- 1 tsp black pepper
- 1 tsp dried thyme
- 1 tsp dried rosemary
- 1 tsp dried basil

Instructions:

1. In a large pan, heat the olive oil over medium heat.

2. Add the onion and garlic and cook until softened, about 5 minutes.

3. Add the chicken and carrots to the pan and cook until the chicken is browned, about 5 minutes.

4. Stir in the chicken broth, diced tomatoes, salt, pepper, thyme, rosemary, and basil.

5. Bring the mixture to a boil and then reduce the heat to low.

6. Cover the pan with a lid and simmer for about 20-25 minutes, or until the chicken is cooked through and the carrots are tender.

7. Serve the chicken and carrot stew with crusty bread.

VEGETABLE

ROASTED KUMARA

Ingredients:

- 2 large Kumara
- 2 tbsp olive oil
- 1 tsp salt
- 1 tsp black pepper

Instructions:

1. Preheat the oven to 200°C (400°F).

2. Wash and peel the Kumara. Cut them into wedges or slices.

3. In a large bowl, toss the Kumara with olive oil, salt, and pepper.

4. Arrange the Kumara in a single layer on a baking sheet.

5. Roast in the oven for 20-25 minutes, or until the Kumara are tender and golden brown.

6. Serve hot as a side dish.

FRIED TARO ROOT

Ingredients:

- 2 large Taro Root
- 1 cup all-purpose flour

- 1 tsp salt
- 1 tsp black pepper
- 1 tsp paprika
- 1 tsp garlic powder
- 1 tsp onion powder
- 1 cup oil for frying

Instructions:

1. Wash and peel the Taro Root. Cut them into thin slices or wedges.

2. In a shallow dish, mix together the flour, salt, pepper, paprika, garlic powder, and onion powder.

3. Dredge the Taro slices in the flour mixture, shaking off any excess.

4. Heat the oil in a large frying pan over medium heat.

5. Fry the Taro slices in the hot oil for 2-3 minutes on each side, or until golden brown and crispy.

6. Drain on paper towels to remove any excess oil.

7. Serve hot as a snack or side dish.

BRAISED KŪMARA

Ingredients:

- 2 large Kūmara
- 2 tbsp butter
- 1 onion, chopped
- 2 garlic cloves, minced
- 1 cup chicken or vegetable broth
- 1 tsp salt

- 1 tsp black pepper

Instructions:

1. Wash and peel the Kūmara. Cut them into 1-inch cubes.

2. In a large saucepan, melt the butter over medium heat. Add the onion and garlic and cook until softened, about 5 minutes.

3. Add the Kūmara to the pan and stir to coat in the butter mixture.

4. Pour in the broth and bring to a simmer. Season with salt and pepper.

5. Cover the pan and cook for 20-25 minutes, or until the Kūmara are tender and the liquid has reduced to a thick sauce.

6. Serve hot as a side dish.

KUMARA CURRY

Ingredients:

- 2 large Kumara
- 2 tbsp oil
- 1 onion, chopped
- 2 garlic cloves, minced
- 1 tsp ginger, grated
- 1 tsp ground cumin
- 1 tsp ground coriander
- 1 tsp turmeric
- 1 tsp paprika
- 1 can (400 ml) coconut milk

- 1 cup water
- 1 tsp salt
- 1 tsp black pepper

Instructions:

1. Wash and peel the Kumara. Cut them into 1-inch cubes.

2. In a large saucepan, heat the oil over medium heat. Add the onion, garlic, and ginger and cook until softened, about 5 minutes.

3. Add the Kumara to the pan and stir to coat in the oil mixture.

4. Stir in the cumin, coriander, turmeric, and paprika and cook for 1-2 minutes until fragrant.

5. Pour in the coconut milk and water and bring to a simmer. Season with salt and pepper.

6. Cover the pan and cook for 20-25 minutes, or until the Kumara are tender and the sauce has thickened.

7. Serve hot with rice or flatbread.

KŪMARA AND CARROT STEW

Ingredients:

- 2 large Kūmara
- 2 large carrots
- 2 tbsp oil
- 1 onion, chopped
- 2 garlic cloves, minced
- 1 tsp ginger, grated

- 1 tsp ground cumin
- 1 tsp ground coriander
- 1 tsp turmeric
- 1 tsp paprika
- 1 can (400 ml) tomato sauce
- 1 cup water
- 1 tsp salt
- 1 tsp black pepper

Instructions:

1. Wash and peel the Kūmara and carrots. Cut them into 1-inch cubes.

2. In a large saucepan, heat the oil over medium heat. Add the onion, garlic, and ginger and cook until softened, about 5 minutes.

3. Add the Kūmara and carrots to the pan and stir to coat in the oil mixture.

4. Stir in the cumin, coriander, turmeric, and paprika and cook for 1-2 minutes until fragrant.

5. Pour in the tomato sauce and water and bring to a simmer. Season with salt and pepper.

6. Cover the pan and cook for 20-25 minutes, or until the vegetables are tender and the sauce has thickened.

7. Serve hot with rice or flatbread.

GRILLED EGGPLANT

Ingredients:

- 2 large eggplants
- 2 tbsp olive oil
- 1 tsp salt
- 1 tsp black pepper

Instructions:

1. Preheat a grill or grill pan to medium-high heat.

2. Wash and slice the eggplants lengthwise into 1/2-inch thick slices.

3. Brush both sides of the eggplant slices with olive oil and season with salt and pepper.

4. Place the eggplant slices on the grill and cook for 3-4 minutes on each side, or until tender and charred.

5. Serve hot as a side dish or in a sandwich or wrap.

FRIED OKRA

Ingredients:

- 1 lb okra
- 1 cup all-purpose flour
- 1 tsp salt
- 1 tsp black pepper
- 1 tsp paprika
- 1 tsp garlic powder
- 1 tsp onion powder
- 1 cup oil for frying

Instructions:

1. Wash and trim the ends of the okra.

2. In a shallow dish, mix together the flour, salt, pepper, paprika, garlic powder, and onion powder.

3. Dredge the okra in the flour mixture, shaking off any excess.

4. Heat the oil in a large frying pan over medium heat.

5. Fry the okra in the hot oil for 2-3 minutes, or until golden brown and crispy.

6. Drain on paper towels to remove any excess oil.

7. Serve hot as a snack or side dish.

BRAISED CAULIFLOWER

Ingredients:

- 1 large head of cauliflower
- 2 tbsp butter
- 1 onion, chopped
- 2 garlic cloves, minced
- 1 cup chicken or vegetable broth
- 1 tsp salt
- 1 tsp black pepper

Instructions:

1. Wash and chop the cauliflower into florets.

2. In a large saucepan, melt the butter over medium heat. Add the onion and garlic and cook until softened, about 5 minutes.

3. Add the cauliflower to the pan and stir to coat in the butter mixture.

4. Pour in the broth and bring to a simmer. Season with salt and pepper.

5. Cover the pan and cook for 15-20 minutes, or until the cauliflower is tender and the liquid has reduced to a thick sauce.

6. Serve hot as a side dish.

GRILLED ZUCCHINI

Ingredients:

- 2 large zucchinis
- 2 tbsp olive oil
- 1 tsp salt
- 1 tsp black pepper

Instructions:

1. Preheat a grill or grill pan to medium-high heat.

2. Wash and slice the zucchinis lengthwise into 1/2-inch thick slices.

3. Brush both sides of the zucchini slices with olive oil and season with salt and pepper.

4. Place the zucchini slices on the grill and cook for 3-4 minutes on each side, or until tender and charred.

5. Serve hot as a side dish or in a sandwich or wrap.

STEAMED BROCCOLI

Ingredients:

- 2 large heads of broccoli
- 1 tsp salt
- 1 tsp black pepper

Instructions:

1. Wash and chop the broccoli into florets.

2. Fill a large saucepan with 1 inch of water and bring to a boil over high heat.

3. Place a steamer basket in the saucepan and add the broccoli florets to the basket.

4. Cover the pan and steam the broccoli for 5-7 minutes, or until tender and bright green.

5. Remove the steamer basket from the saucepan and transfer the broccoli to a serving dish.

6. Season with salt and pepper to taste.

7. Serve hot as a side dish.

SIDE DISHES

FRIED RICE

Ingredients:

- 2 cups of Rice
- 1 tablespoon of Oil
- 1 Onion, diced
- 1 Carrot, diced
- 1 cup of Peas
- 1 teaspoon of Salt
- 1 tablespoon of Soy Sauce

Instructions:

1. Cook the rice according to the package instructions and set aside.

2. In a pan, heat the oil over medium heat. Add the onion and cook until softened, about 3 minutes.

3. Add the carrot and peas to the pan and cook for another 2 minutes.

4. Add the cooked rice to the pan and stir to combine with the vegetables.

5. Season with salt and soy sauce, and continue to stir until the ingredients are well mixed.

6. Serve hot and enjoy your delicious fried rice.

ROASTED KUMARA

Ingredients:

- 2 large Kumara (Sweet Potatoes), peeled and diced
- 2 tablespoons of Olive Oil
- 1 teaspoon of Salt
- 1 teaspoon of Paprika

Instructions:

1. Preheat the oven to 200°C (400°F).

2. In a large bowl, toss the diced kumara with olive oil, salt, and paprika until evenly coated.

3. Transfer the kumara to a baking sheet and spread them out in a single layer.

4. Roast in the preheated oven for 25-30 minutes, or until the kumara is tender and lightly browned.

5. Serve hot as a tasty side dish with your favorite meal.

MASHED POTATOES

Ingredients:

- 4 large Potatoes, peeled and diced
- 1/4 cup of Milk
- 2 tablespoons of Butter
- 1 teaspoon of Salt
- 1/4 teaspoon of Black Pepper

Instructions:

1. Place the diced potatoes in a large pot and cover with water. Bring to a boil and cook until the potatoes are tender, about 20 minutes.

2. Drain the potatoes and return them to the pot.

3. Add the milk, butter, salt, and pepper to the pot and mash the potatoes until they are smooth and creamy.

4. Taste and adjust the seasoning as needed.

5. Serve hot as a comforting and delicious side dish.

FRIED PLANTAINS

Ingredients:

- 2 ripe Plantains, peeled and sliced
- 1 cup of Vegetable Oil for frying
- 1 teaspoon of Salt

Instructions:

1. In a large pan, heat the vegetable oil over medium heat.

2. Add the sliced plantains to the pan and fry until they are golden brown on both sides, about 2-3 minutes per side.

3. Remove the plantains from the pan and place them on a paper towel to drain any excess oil.

4. Sprinkle with salt and serve hot as a tasty and sweet side dish.

GRILLED VEGETABLES

Ingredients:

- 1 large Bell Pepper, sliced
- 1 large Zucchini, sliced
- 1 large Eggplant, sliced
- 2 tablespoons of Olive Oil
- 1 teaspoon of Salt
- 1/4 teaspoon of Black Pepper

Instructions:

1. Preheat a grill or grill pan to medium-high heat.

2. In a large bowl, toss the bell pepper, zucchini, and eggplant with olive oil, salt, and pepper until evenly coated.

3. Place the vegetables on the preheated grill and cook until they are tender and lightly charred, about 5-7 minutes per side.

4. Serve hot as a healthy and delicious side dish.

BAKED BEANS

Ingredients:

- 2 cans of Baked Beans
- 1 Onion, diced
- 1 tablespoon of Brown Sugar
- 1 tablespoon of Mustard
- 1 tablespoon of Vinegar
- 1 tablespoon of Worcestershire Sauce

Instructions:

1. Preheat the oven to 180°C (350°F).

2. In a large bowl, mix together the baked beans, onion, brown sugar, mustard, vinegar, and Worcestershire sauce.

3. Transfer the mixture to a baking dish and bake in the preheated oven for 25-30 minutes, or until heated through and slightly caramelized on top.

4. Serve hot as a classic and hearty side dish.

FRIED CASSAVA

Ingredients:

- 2 large Cassava, peeled and sliced
- 1 cup of Vegetable Oil for frying
- 1 teaspoon of Salt

Instructions:

1. In a large pan, heat the vegetable oil over medium heat.

2. Add the sliced cassava to the pan and fry until they are golden brown on both sides, about 2-3 minutes per side.

3. Remove the cassava from the pan and place them on a paper towel to drain any excess oil.

4. Sprinkle with salt and serve hot as a delicious and starchy side dish.

ROASTED SWEET POTATO

Ingredients:

- 2 large Sweet Potatoes, peeled and diced
- 2 tablespoons of Olive Oil
- 1 teaspoon of Salt
- 1 teaspoon of Paprika

Instructions:

1. Preheat the oven to 200°C (400°F).

2. In a large bowl, toss the diced sweet potatoes with olive oil, salt, and paprika until evenly coated.

3. Transfer the sweet potatoes to a baking sheet and spread them out in a single layer.

4. Roast in the preheated oven for 25-30 minutes, or until the sweet potatoes are tender and lightly browned.

5. Serve hot as a nutritious and delicious side dish with your favorite meal.

STEAMED CARROTS

Ingredients:

- 4 large Carrots, peeled and sliced
- 1 tablespoon of Butter
- 1 teaspoon of Salt
- 1/4 teaspoon of Black Pepper

Instructions:

1. Fill a large pot with about 2 inches of water and bring to a boil.

2. Place the sliced carrots in a steamer basket and place the basket over the boiling water.

3. Cover the pot and steam the carrots until they are tender, about 10-12 minutes.

4. In a small saucepan, melt the butter over low heat.

5. Remove the carrots from the steamer basket and transfer them to a serving dish.

6. Pour the melted butter over the carrots, sprinkle with salt and pepper, and serve hot as a healthy and flavorful side dish.

GRILLED CORN ON THE COB

Ingredients:

- 4 ears of Corn, husks removed
- 2 tablespoons of Butter, melted
- 1 teaspoon of Salt
- 1/4 teaspoon of Black Pepper

Instructions:

1. Preheat a grill or grill pan to medium-high heat.

2. Brush the corn with melted butter and season with salt and pepper.

3. Place the corn on the preheated grill and cook, turning occasionally, until the kernels are tender and slightly charred, about 10-15 minutes.

4. Serve hot as a delicious and sweet side dish with your favorite meal.

BREADS

FRIED BREAD

Ingredients:

- 3 cups all-purpose flour
- 1 teaspoon salt
- 1 teaspoon sugar
- 2 teaspoons active dry yeast
- 1 cup warm water
- Vegetable oil for frying

Instructions:

1. In a large mixing bowl, combine the flour, salt, and sugar. Mix well.

2. In a separate bowl, dissolve the yeast in the warm water. Let it sit for 5 minutes or until it becomes frothy.

3. Add the yeast mixture to the flour mixture and stir until a dough forms. Knead the dough on a floured surface for 10 minutes.

4. Place the dough in a greased bowl and cover with a clean cloth. Let it rise in a warm place for 1 hour or until doubled in size.

5. On a floured surface, roll out the dough to about 1/4 inch thickness. Cut into desired shapes.

6. In a large frying pan, heat the vegetable oil over medium heat. Fry the bread until golden brown on both sides, about 2-3 minutes per side.

7. Drain on paper towels and serve hot.

SWEET POTATO BISCUITS

Ingredients:

- 2 cups all-purpose flour
- 2 teaspoons baking powder
- 1/2 teaspoon salt
- 1/4 cup unsalted butter, chilled and cubed
- 1 cup mashed sweet potato
- 1/2 cup milk

Instructions:

1. Preheat the oven to 425°F (220°C). Line a baking sheet with parchment paper.

2. In a large mixing bowl, whisk together the flour, baking powder, and salt.

3. Using a pastry cutter or your hands, cut in the butter until the mixture resembles coarse crumbs.

4. Add the mashed sweet potato and milk to the mixture and stir until just combined.

5. On a floured surface, roll out the dough to about 1/2 inch thickness. Cut into desired shapes.

6. Place the biscuits on the prepared baking sheet and bake for 15-20 minutes or until golden brown.

7. Serve warm with butter and honey if desired.

KUMARA BREAD

Ingredients:

- 2 cups all-purpose flour
- 1 teaspoon baking powder
- 1/2 teaspoon baking soda
- 1/2 teaspoon salt
- 1/2 cup unsalted butter, melted
- 1 cup brown sugar
- 2 large eggs
- 1 cup mashed kumara (sweet potato)
- 1/2 cup milk

Instructions:

1. Preheat the oven to 350°F (180°C). Grease a 9x5 inch loaf pan.

2. In a large mixing bowl, whisk together the flour, baking powder, baking soda, and salt.

3. In a separate bowl, whisk together the melted butter, brown sugar, eggs, mashed kumara, and milk.

4. Add the wet ingredients to the dry ingredients and stir until just combined.

5. Pour the batter into the prepared loaf pan and bake for 45-50 minutes or until a toothpick inserted into the center comes out clean.

6. Let the bread cool in the pan for 10 minutes before transferring to a wire rack to cool completely.

TARO ROOT BREAD

Ingredients:

- 2 cups all-purpose flour
- 1 teaspoon baking powder
- 1/2 teaspoon baking soda
- 1/2 teaspoon salt
- 1/2 cup unsalted butter, melted
- 1 cup brown sugar
- 2 large eggs
- 1 cup mashed taro root
- 1/2 cup milk

Instructions:

1. Preheat the oven to 350°F (180°C). Grease a 9x5 inch loaf pan.

2. In a large mixing bowl, whisk together the flour, baking powder, baking soda, and salt.

3. In a separate bowl, whisk together the melted butter, brown sugar, eggs, mashed taro root, and milk.

4. Add the wet ingredients to the dry ingredients and stir until just combined.

5. Pour the batter into the prepared loaf pan and bake for 45-50 minutes or until a toothpick inserted into the center comes out clean.

6. Let the bread cool in the pan for 10 minutes before transferring to a wire rack to cool completely.

CORNBREAD

Ingredients:

- 1 cup all-purpose flour
- 1 cup cornmeal
- 2 teaspoons baking powder
- 1/2 teaspoon baking soda
- 1/2 teaspoon salt
- 1/4 cup unsalted butter, melted
- 1/2 cup sugar
- 2 large eggs
- 1 cup buttermilk

Instructions:

1. Preheat the oven to 425°F (220°C). Grease an 8x8 inch baking dish.

2. In a large mixing bowl, whisk together the flour, cornmeal, baking powder, baking soda, and salt.

3. In a separate bowl, whisk together the melted butter, sugar, eggs, and buttermilk.

4. Add the wet ingredients to the dry ingredients and stir until just combined.

5. Pour the batter into the prepared baking dish and bake for 20-25 minutes or until a toothpick inserted into the center comes out clean.

6. Let the cornbread cool in the pan for 10 minutes before slicing and serving.

BANANA BREAD

Ingredients:

- 2 cups all-purpose flour
- 1 teaspoon baking powder
- 1/2 teaspoon baking soda
- 1/2 teaspoon salt
- 1/2 cup unsalted butter, melted
- 1 cup brown sugar
- 2 large eggs
- 3 ripe bananas, mashed
- 1/2 cup buttermilk

Instructions:

1. Preheat the oven to 350°F (180°C). Grease a 9x5 inch loaf pan.

2. In a large mixing bowl, whisk together the flour, baking powder, baking soda, and salt.

3. In a separate bowl, whisk together the melted butter, brown sugar, eggs, mashed bananas, and buttermilk.

4. Add the wet ingredients to the dry ingredients and stir until just combined.

5. Pour the batter into the prepared loaf pan and bake for 45-50 minutes or until a toothpick inserted into the center comes out clean.

6. Let the bread cool in the pan for 10 minutes before transferring to a wire rack to cool completely.

POTATO BREAD

Ingredients:

- 2 cups all-purpose flour
- 1 teaspoon baking powder
- 1/2 teaspoon baking soda
- 1/2 teaspoon salt
- 1/2 cup unsalted butter, melted
- 1 cup brown sugar
- 2 large eggs
- 1 cup mashed potatoes
- 1/2 cup buttermilk

Instructions:

1. Preheat the oven to 350°F (180°C). Grease a 9x5 inch loaf pan.

2. In a large mixing bowl, whisk together the flour, baking powder, baking soda, and salt.

3. In a separate bowl, whisk together the melted butter, brown sugar, eggs, mashed potatoes, and buttermilk.

4. Add the wet ingredients to the dry ingredients and stir until just combined.

5. Pour the batter into the prepared loaf pan and bake for 45-50 minutes or until a toothpick inserted into the center comes out clean.

6. Let the bread cool in the pan for 10 minutes before transferring to a wire rack to cool completely.

CARROT BREAD

Ingredients:

- 2 cups all-purpose flour
- 1 teaspoon baking powder
- 1/2 teaspoon baking soda
- 1/2 teaspoon salt
- 1/2 cup unsalted butter, melted
- 1 cup brown sugar
- 2 large eggs
- 1 cup grated carrots
- 1/2 cup buttermilk

Instructions:

1. Preheat the oven to 350°F (180°C). Grease a 9x5 inch loaf pan.

2. In a large mixing bowl, whisk together the flour, baking powder, baking soda, and salt.

3. In a separate bowl, whisk together the melted butter, brown sugar, eggs, grated carrots, and buttermilk.

4. Add the wet ingredients to the dry ingredients and stir until just combined.

5. Pour the batter into the prepared loaf pan and bake for 45-50 minutes or until a toothpick inserted into the center comes out clean.

6. Let the bread cool in the pan for 10 minutes before transferring to a wire rack to cool completely.

PUMPKIN BREAD

Ingredients:

- 2 cups all-purpose flour
- 1 teaspoon baking powder
- 1/2 teaspoon baking soda
- 1/2 teaspoon salt
- 1/2 cup unsalted butter, melted
- 1 cup brown sugar
- 2 large eggs
- 1 cup pumpkin puree
- 1/2 cup buttermilk

Instructions:

1. Preheat the oven to 350°F (180°C). Grease a 9x5 inch loafpan.

2. In a large mixing bowl, whisk together the flour, baking powder, baking soda, and salt.

3. In a separate bowl, whisk together the melted butter, brown sugar, eggs, pumpkin puree, and buttermilk.

4. Add the wet ingredients to the dry ingredients and stir until just combined.

5. Pour the batter into the prepared loaf pan and bake for 45-50 minutes or until a toothpick inserted into the center comes out clean.

6. Let the bread cool in the pan for 10 minutes before transferring to a wire rack to cool completely.

ZUCCHINI BREAD

Ingredients:

- 2 cups all-purpose flour
- 1 teaspoon baking powder
- 1/2 teaspoon baking soda
- 1/2 teaspoon salt
- 1/2 cup unsalted butter, melted
- 1 cup brown sugar
- 2 large eggs
- 1 cup grated zucchini
- 1/2 cup buttermilk

Instructions:

1. Preheat the oven to 350°F (180°C). Grease a 9x5 inch loaf pan.

2. In a large mixing bowl, whisk together the flour, baking powder, baking soda, and salt.

3. In a separate bowl, whisk together the melted butter, brown sugar, eggs, grated zucchini, and buttermilk.

4. Add the wet ingredients to the dry ingredients and stir until just combined.

5. Pour the batter into the prepared loaf pan and bake for 45-50 minutes or until a toothpick inserted into the center comes out clean.

6. Let the bread cool in the pan for 10 minutes before transferring to a wire rack to cool completely.

SAUCES

KUMARA AND BACON SAUCE

Ingredients:

- 1 large Kumara (sweet potato), peeled and diced
- 6 strips of bacon, diced
- 1 onion, chopped
- 1 clove of garlic, minced
- 1/2 cup chicken broth
- 1/2 cup heavy cream
- Salt and pepper to taste

Instructions:

1. In a large pan, cook the bacon over medium heat until crispy. Remove the bacon from the pan and set aside. Reserve 1 tablespoon of the bacon grease in the pan.

2. Add the chopped onion to the pan and cook until softened, about 5 minutes. Add the minced garlic and cook for an additional minute.

3. Add the diced kumara to the pan and stir to coat with the bacon grease. Cook for 5 minutes, until the kumara begins to soften.

4. Pour in the chicken broth and bring to a boil. Reduce the heat to low and let simmer for 10 minutes, until the kumara is fully cooked and soft.

5. Use an immersion blender or transfer the mixture to a blender to puree until smooth. Return the puree to the pan and stir in the heavy cream and cooked bacon.

6. Season with salt and pepper to taste. Serve warm.

TARO ROOT SAUCE

Ingredients:

- 2 large taro roots, peeled and diced
- 1 onion, chopped
- 1 clove of garlic, minced
- 1 cup chicken broth
- 1 cup coconut milk
- Salt and pepper to taste

Instructions:

1. In a large pan, cook the chopped onion over medium heat until softened, about 5 minutes. Add the minced garlic and cook for an additional minute.

2. Add the diced taro root to the pan and stir to coat with the onions. Cook for 5 minutes, until the taro root begins to soften.

3. Pour in the chicken broth and bring to a boil. Reduce the heat to low and let simmer for 10 minutes, until the taro root is fully cooked and soft.

4. Use an immersion blender or transfer the mixture to a blender to puree until smooth. Return the puree to the pan and stir in the coconut milk.

5. Season with salt and pepper to taste. Serve warm.

KŪMARA GRAVY

Ingredients:

- 2 large Kumara (sweet potatoes), peeled and diced
- 1 onion, chopped
- 1 clove of garlic, minced
- 2 cups chicken broth
- 1/2 cup heavy cream
- 2 tablespoons cornstarch
- Salt and pepper to taste

Instructions:

1. In a large pan, cook the chopped onion over medium heat until softened, about 5 minutes. Add the minced garlic and cook for an additional minute.

2. Add the diced kumara to the pan and stir to coat with the onions. Cook for 5 minutes, until the kumara begins to soften.

3. Pour in the chicken broth and bring to a boil. Reduce the heat to low and let simmer for 10 minutes, until the kumara is fully cooked and soft.

4. In a small bowl, whisk together the heavy cream and cornstarch. Stir the mixture into the pan with the kumara and broth.

5. Increase the heat to medium and bring the mixture to a boil, stirring constantly. Once the mixture has thickened, reduce the heat to low and let simmer for 5 minutes.

6. Season with salt and pepper to taste. Serve warm as a gravy for roasted meats.

TOMATO SAUCE

Ingredients:

- 2 pounds ripe tomatoes, chopped
- 1 onion, chopped
- 1 clove of garlic, minced
- 2 tablespoons olive oil
- 1 teaspoon sugar
- 1 teaspoon dried basil
- Salt and pepper to taste

Instructions:

1. In a large pan, heat the olive oil over medium heat. Add the chopped onion and cook until softened, about 5 minutes. Add the minced garlic and cook for an additional minute.

2. Add the chopped tomatoes to the pan and stir to combine with the onions and garlic. Cook for 10 minutes, until the tomatoes begin to soften and release their juice.

3. Use an immersion blender or transfer the mixture to a blender to puree until smooth. Return the puree to the pan.

4. Stir in the sugar and dried basil. Season with salt and pepper to taste.

5. Let the sauce simmer for an additional 10 minutes, until thickened to your desired consistency. Serve warm over pasta or as a base for pizza or stews.

SPICY MAYO

Ingredients:

- 1 cup mayonnaise
- 1 tablespoon sriracha sauce
- 1 teaspoon lemon juice
- 1 clove of garlic, minced
- Salt and pepper to taste

Instructions:

1. In a small bowl, whisk together the mayonnaise, sriracha sauce, lemon juice, and minced garlic until well combined.

2. Season with salt and pepper to taste.

3. Chill the sauce in the refrigerator for at least 30 minutes to allow the flavors to meld.

4. Serve the spicy mayo as a dipping sauce or as a spread for sandwiches and burgers.

PAPAYA CHUTNEY

Ingredients:

- 1 ripe papaya, peeled, seeded, and diced
- 1/2 onion, chopped
- 1/2 cup white wine vinegar
- 1/2 cup sugar
- 1 teaspoon mustard seeds
- 1 teaspoon cumin seeds
- 1 teaspoon salt

Instructions:

1. In a large pan, combine the diced papaya, chopped onion, white wine vinegar, sugar, mustard seeds, cumin seeds, and salt.

2. Bring the mixture to a boil over medium heat, then reduce the heat to low and let simmer for 20-30 minutes, until the mixture has thickened and the papaya is soft.

3. Use an immersion blender or transfer the mixture to a blender to puree until smooth.

4. Chill the chutney in the refrigerator for at least 30 minutes to allow the flavors to meld.

5. Serve the papaya chutney as a condiment or as a sauce for grilled meats and vegetables.

MINT SAUCE

Ingredients:

- 1/2 cup fresh mint leaves, chopped
- 1/4 cup white wine vinegar
- 2 tablespoons sugar
- 1/2 teaspoon salt

Instructions:

1. In a small bowl, whisk together the chopped mint leaves, white wine vinegar, sugar, and salt until the sugar has dissolved.

2. Chill the sauce in the refrigerator for at least 30 minutes to allow the flavors to meld.

3. Serve the mint sauce as a condiment or as a sauce for grilled meats and vegetables.

PLUM SAUCE

Ingredients:

- 2 pounds ripe plums, pitted and chopped
- 1/2 onion, chopped
- 1/2 cup white wine vinegar
- 1/2 cup brown sugar
- 1 teaspoon ginger, grated
- 1 teaspoon garlic, minced
- 1 teaspoon salt

Instructions:

1. In a large pan, combine the chopped plums, chopped onion, white wine vinegar, brown sugar, grated ginger, minced garlic, and salt.

2. Bring the mixture to a boil over medium heat, then reduce the heat to low and let simmer for 20-30 minutes, until the mixture has thickened and the plums are soft.

3. Use an immersion blender or transfer the mixture to a blender to puree until smooth.

4. Chill the sauce in the refrigerator for at least 30 minutes to allow the flavors to meld.

5. Serve the plum sauce as a condiment or as a sauce for grilled meats and vegetables.

APPLE SAUCE

Ingredients:

- 2 pounds apples, peeled, cored, and chopped
- 1/2 cup water

- 1/4 cup sugar
- 1 teaspoon cinnamon
- 1/2 teaspoon nutmeg

Instructions:

1. In a large pan, combine the chopped apples, water, sugar, cinnamon, and nutmeg.

2. Bring the mixture to a boil over medium heat, then reduce the heat to low and let simmer for 20-30 minutes, until the apples are soft and the mixture has thickened.

3. Use an immersion blender or transfer the mixture to a blender to puree until smooth.

4. Chill the sauce in the refrigerator for at least 30 minutes to allow the flavors to meld.

5. Serve the apple sauce as a side dish or as a topping for pancakes, waffles, and oatmeal.

CRANBERRY SAUCE

Ingredients:

- 2 cups fresh cranberries
- 1 cup sugar
- 1 cup water
- 1 teaspoon orange zest
- 1 teaspoon cinnamon

Instructions:

1. In a large pan, combine the cranberries, sugar, water, orange zest, and cinnamon.

2. Bring the mixture to a boil over medium heat, then reduce the heat to low and let simmer for 20-30 minutes, until the cranberries have burst and the mixture has thickened.

3. Use an immersion blender or transfer the mixture to a blender to puree until smooth.

4. Chill the sauce in the refrigerator for at least 30 minutes to allow the flavors to meld.

5. Serve the cranberry sauce as a side dish or as a topping for roasted meats, especially during the holiday season.

DESSERTS

FRIED BREADFRUIT WITH HONEY

Ingredients:

- 1 large breadfruit, peeled and sliced
- 1 cup flour
- 2 teaspoons baking powder
- 1 teaspoon salt
- 1/2 cup water
- 1 cup oil for frying
- 1/2 cup honey

Instructions:

1. In a large mixing bowl, whisk together the flour, baking powder, and salt. Add water and mix until batter forms.

2. Heat oil in a large frying pan over medium-high heat. Dip each breadfruit slice into the batter, then carefully place into the hot oil. Fry until golden brown on both sides, about 2-3 minutes per side.

3. Remove from heat and drain on paper towels. Serve with honey drizzled on top.

SWEET POTATO PUDDING

Ingredients:

- 2 large sweet potatoes, peeled and mashed
- 1/2 cup sugar
- 2 eggs
- 1/2 cup milk

- 1 teaspoon vanilla extract
- 1/2 teaspoon ground cinnamon
- 1/4 teaspoon ground nutmeg

Instructions:

1. Preheat oven to 350°F. Grease a 9x9 inch baking dish.

2. In a large mixing bowl, whisk together the mashed sweet potatoes, sugar, eggs, milk, vanilla extract, cinnamon, and nutmeg until smooth.

3. Pour mixture into the prepared baking dish and bake for 30-35 minutes, or until set and lightly golden on top.

KŪMARA AND GINGER CAKE

Ingredients:

- 1 1/2 cups kūmara, peeled and grated
- 1 cup flour
- 1 teaspoon baking powder
- 1/2 teaspoon baking soda
- 1/2 teaspoon salt
- 1 teaspoon ground ginger
- 1/2 cup sugar
- 2 eggs
- 1/2 cup oil
- 1/2 cup milk

Instructions:

1. Preheat oven to 350°F. Grease a 9x9 inch baking dish.

2. In a large mixing bowl, whisk together the flour, baking powder, baking soda, salt, and ginger.

3. In a separate bowl, whisk together the grated kūmara, sugar, eggs, oil, and milk. Add the wet ingredients to the dry ingredients and mix until just combined.

4. Pour mixture into the prepared baking dish and bake for 35-40 minutes, or until a toothpick inserted into the center comes out clean.

TARO ROOT PIE

Ingredients:

- 1 large taro root, peeled and sliced
- 1 pie crust
- 1/2 cup sugar
- 2 tablespoons cornstarch
- 1 teaspoon ground cinnamon
- 1/4 teaspoon ground nutmeg
- 1/2 cup water

Instructions:

1. Preheat oven to 375°F. Roll out pie crust and place into a 9 inch pie dish.

2. In a saucepan over medium heat, whisk together the sugar, cornstarch, cinnamon, nutmeg, and water. Add the sliced taro root and cook until mixture thickens, about 5 minutes.

3. Pour mixture into the prepared pie crust and smooth out evenly. Bake for 25-30 minutes, or until the crust is golden and the filling is set.

BANANA AND KUMARA CAKE

Ingredients:

- 1 1/2 cups kūmara, peeled and grated
- 2 ripe bananas, mashed
- 1 1/2 cups flour
- 1 teaspoon baking powder
- 1/2 teaspoon baking soda
- 1/2 teaspoon salt
- 1/2 cup sugar
- 2 eggs
- 1/2 cup oil
- 1/2 cup milk

Instructions:

1. Preheat oven to 350°F. Grease a 9x9 inch baking dish.

2. In a large mixing bowl, whisk together the flour, baking powder, baking soda, salt, and sugar.

3. In a separate bowl, whisk together the grated kūmara, mashed bananas, eggs, oil, and milk. Add the wet ingredients to the dry ingredients and mix until just combined.

4. Pour mixture into the prepared baking dish and bake for 35-40 minutes, or until a toothpick inserted into the center comes out clean.

PUMPKIN PIE

Ingredients:

- 1 pie crust
- 1 can pumpkin puree

- 3/4 cup sugar
- 1 teaspoon ground cinnamon
- 1/2 teaspoon ground nutmeg
- 1/4 teaspoon ground ginger
- 1/4 teaspoon ground cloves
- 2 eggs
- 1 cup heavy cream

Instructions:

1. Preheat oven to 375°F. Roll out pie crust and place into a 9 inch pie dish.

2. In a large mixing bowl, whisk together the pumpkin puree, sugar, cinnamon, nutmeg, ginger, cloves, eggs, and heavy cream until smooth.

3. Pour mixture into the prepared pie crust and smooth out evenly. Bake for 45-50 minutes, or until the crust is golden and the filling is set.

FRIED PLANTAINS WITH CINNAMON SUGAR

Ingredients:

- 2 ripe plantains, sliced
- 1/2 cup sugar
- 1 teaspoon ground cinnamon
- 1 cup oil for frying

Instructions:

1. In a small mixing bowl, whisk together the sugar and cinnamon to make the cinnamon sugar.

2. Heat oil in a large frying pan over medium-high heat. Dip each plantain slice into the cinnamon sugar, then carefully place into the hot oil. Fry until golden brown on both sides, about 2-3 minutes per side.

3. Remove from heat and drain on paper towels. Serve hot.

SWEET POTATO AND CINNAMON MUFFINS

Ingredients:

- 1 cup sweet potato, peeled and grated
- 1 1/2 cups flour
- 1 teaspoon baking powder
- 1/2 teaspoon baking soda
- 1/2 teaspoon salt
- 1 teaspoon ground cinnamon
- 1/2 cup sugar
- 2 eggs
- 1/2 cup oil
- 1/2 cup milk

Instructions:

1. Preheat oven to 375°F. Line a muffin tin with muffin cups.

2. In a large mixing bowl, whisk together the flour, baking powder, baking soda, salt, and cinnamon.

3. In a separate bowl, whisk together the grated sweet potato, sugar, eggs, oil, and milk. Add the wet ingredients to the dry ingredients and mix until just combined.

4. Fill each muffin cup about 2/3 full with batter. Bake for 20-25 minutes, or until a toothpick inserted into the center of a muffin comes out clean.

BAKED APPLES WITH RAISINS

Ingredients:

- 6 large apples
- 1/2 cup raisins
- 1/2 cup brown sugar
- 1 teaspoon ground cinnamon
- 1/4 teaspoon ground nutmeg
- 1/2 cup water
- 1 tablespoon butter

Instructions:

1. Preheat oven to 375°F. Grease a 9x9 inch baking dish.

2. Core the apples and place them in the prepared baking dish. Fill the center of each apple with raisins.

3. In a small mixing bowl, whisk together the brown sugar, cinnamon, and nutmeg. Sprinkle mixture over the apples and raisins.

4. Pour water into the bottom of the baking dish. Dot the top of the apples with butter. Cover with foil and bake for 30-35 minutes, or until apples are tender.

CARROT CAKE

Ingredients:

- 2 cups grated carrots
- 1 1/2 cups flour

- 1 teaspoon baking powder
- 1/2 teaspoon baking soda
- 1/2 teaspoon salt
- 1 teaspoon ground cinnamon
- 1/2 cup sugar
- 2 eggs
- 1/2 cup oil
- 1/2 cup milk

Instructions:

1. Preheat oven to 375°F. Grease a 9x9 inch baking dish.

2. In a large mixing bowl, whisk together the flour, baking powder, baking soda, salt, and cinnamon.

3. In a separate bowl, whisk together the grated carrots, sugar, eggs, oil, and milk. Add the wet ingredients to the dry ingredients and mix until just combined.

4. Pour mixture into the prepared baking dish and bake for 35-40 minutes, or until a toothpick inserted into the center comes out clean.

BEVERAGES

KUMARA JUICE

Ingredients:

- 2 medium-sized kumara
- 2 cups of water
- 1 tsp honey (optional)
- 1/2 lemon, juiced

Instructions:

1. Wash and peel the kumara.

2. Cut the kumara into small pieces and place in a blender.

3. Add the water, honey, and lemon juice to the blender.

4. Blend until smooth and strain through a fine mesh sieve into a glass.

5. Serve immediately, garnished with a lemon wedge if desired.

TARO ROOT SMOOTHIE

Ingredients:

- 2 medium-sized taro roots
- 1 cup of coconut milk
- 1 banana
- 1 tsp honey (optional)
- 1 tsp vanilla extract

Instructions:

1. Wash and peel the taro roots.

2. Cut the taro roots into small pieces and place in a blender.

3. Add the coconut milk, banana, honey, and vanilla extract to the blender.

4. Blend until smooth and pour into glasses.

5. Serve immediately, garnished with a sprinkle of cinnamon if desired.

SWEET POTATO LATTE

Ingredients:

- 1 medium-sized sweet potato
- 2 cups of milk
- 1 tsp cinnamon
- 1 tsp vanilla extract
- 1 tbsp honey (optional)

Instructions:

1. Wash and peel the sweet potato.

2. Cut the sweet potato into small pieces and place in a blender.

3. Add the milk, cinnamon, vanilla extract, and honey to the blender.

4. Blend until smooth and pour into a saucepan.

5. Heat the mixture over medium heat until hot, then pour into mugs.

6. Serve immediately, garnished with a sprinkle of cinnamon if desired.

KUMARA AND GINGER TEA

Ingredients:

- 1 medium-sized kumara
- 1 inch of fresh ginger, peeled and grated
- 4 cups of water
- 1 tsp honey (optional)
- 1/2 lemon, juiced

Instructions:

1. Wash and peel the kumara.

2. Cut the kumara into small pieces and place in a saucepan.

3. Add the grated ginger, water, honey, and lemon juice to the saucepan.

4. Bring the mixture to a boil, then reduce heat and let simmer for 10 minutes.

5. Strain the mixture through a fine mesh sieve into a glass.

6. Serve immediately, garnished with a lemon wedge if desired.

ROASTED MAORI POTATO DRINK

Ingredients:

- 2 medium-sized Maori potatoes
- 2 cups of water
- 1 tsp honey (optional)
- 1/2 lemon, juiced

Instructions:

1. Preheat the oven to 400°F (200°C).

2. Wash and peel the Maori potatoes.

3. Cut the Maori potatoes into small pieces and place on a baking sheet.

4. Roast the Maori potatoes for 20 minutes, or until soft and slightly browned.

5. Place the roasted Maori potatoes in a blender, along with the water, honey, and lemon juice.

6. Blend until smooth and strain through a fine mesh sieve into a glass.

7. Serve immediately, garnished with a lemon wedge if desired.

PINEAPPLE AND KŪMARA JUICE

Ingredients:

- 1 medium-sized kumara
- 1 cup of pineapple, cubed
- 2 cups of water

- 1 tsp honey (optional)
- 1/2 lemon, juiced

Instructions:

1. Wash and peel the kumara.

2. Cut the kumara into small pieces and place in a blender.

3. Add the pineapple, water, honey, and lemon juice to the blender.

4. Blend until smooth and strain through a fine mesh sieve into a glass.

5. Serve immediately, garnished with a pineapple wedge if desired.

SWEET POTATO AND CINNAMON SHAKE

Ingredients:

- 1 medium-sized sweet potato
- 1 cup of milk
- 1 banana
- 1 tsp cinnamon
- 1 tsp vanilla extract
- 1 tbsp honey (optional)

Instructions:

1. Wash and peel the sweet potato.

2. Cut the sweet potato into small pieces and place in a blender.

3. Add the milk, banana, cinnamon, vanilla extract, and honey to the blender.

4. Blend until smooth and pour into glasses.

5. Serve immediately, garnished with a sprinkle of cinnamon if desired.

TARO ROOT MILK

Ingredients:

- 2 medium-sized taro roots
- 2 cups of milk
- 1 tsp cinnamon
- 1 tsp vanilla extract
- 1 tbsp honey (optional)

Instructions:

1. Wash and peel the taro roots.

2. Cut the taro roots into small pieces and place in a blender.

3. Add the milk, cinnamon, vanilla extract, and honey to the blender.

4. Blend until smooth and strain through a fine mesh sieve into a glass.

5. Serve immediately, garnished with a sprinkle of cinnamon if desired.

KUMARA AND CARROT JUICE

Ingredients:

- 1 medium-sized kumara
- 2 medium-sized carrots
- 2 cups of water
- 1 tsp honey (optional)
- 1/2 lemon, juiced

Instructions:

1. Wash and peel the kumara and carrots.

2. Cut the kumara and carrots into small pieces and place in a blender.

3. Add the water, honey, and lemon juice to the blender.

4. Blend until smooth and strain through a fine mesh sieve into a glass.

5. Serve immediately, garnished with a lemon wedge if desired.

SWEET POTATO AND VANILLA SMOOTHIE

Ingredients:

- 1 medium-sized sweet potato
- 1 cup of coconut milk
- 1 banana
- 1 tsp vanilla extract
- 1 tbsp honey (optional)

Instructions:

1. Wash and peel the sweet potato.

2. Cut the sweet potato into small pieces and place in a blender.

3. Add the coconut milk, banana, vanilla extract, and honey to the blender.

4. Blend until smooth and pour into glasses.

5. Serve immediately, garnished with a sprinkle of cinnamon if desired.

RECIPES LIST

STARTERS

SNACKS

SOUPS

STEWS

SEAFOOD

LAMB

PORK

POULTRY

VEGETABLES

SIDE DISHES

BREADS

SAUCES

DESSERTS

BEVERAGES

Printed in Dunstable, United Kingdom

64569912R10087